A MIDSOMMAR NIGHT'S DREAME

Jabberwoke Pocket Occult Collection

~

Crystal Gazing by Frater Achad

Heavenly Bridegrooms by Ida Craddock

Moonchild by Aleister Crowley

The Kybalion by Three Initiates

The So-Called Occult by Carl Jung

The Great God Pan by Arthur Machen

The Witch Cult by Margaret Murray

The Book of Lies by Frater Perdurabo

A Midsommar Night's Dreame by William Shakespeare

Satan: A Novel by Mark Twain

~

A Midſommer nights dreame.

As it hath beene ſundry times pub-
likely acted, by the *Right Honoura-*
ble, the Lord Chamberlaine his
ſeruants.

VVritten by VVilliam Shakeſpeare.

Printed by *Jabberwoke,* 2021
San Francisco

MidsommarNights.com

Fae Folk:
Oberon, King of Faeries
Titania, Queen of Fairies
Robin "Puck" Goodfellow

Fairie Handmaids:
Pease-Blossom
Cobweb
Moth
Mustardseed

The Lovers:
Helena, who is in love with:
Demetrius, who is in love with:
Helena, who is in love with:
Lysander, who loves Helena in turn.

The Players:
Quince, the Carpenter,
Snug, the Ioiner,
Bottom, The VVeauer,
Starueling, the Tailer,
Flute, the Bellows-mender, &
Snout, the Tinker

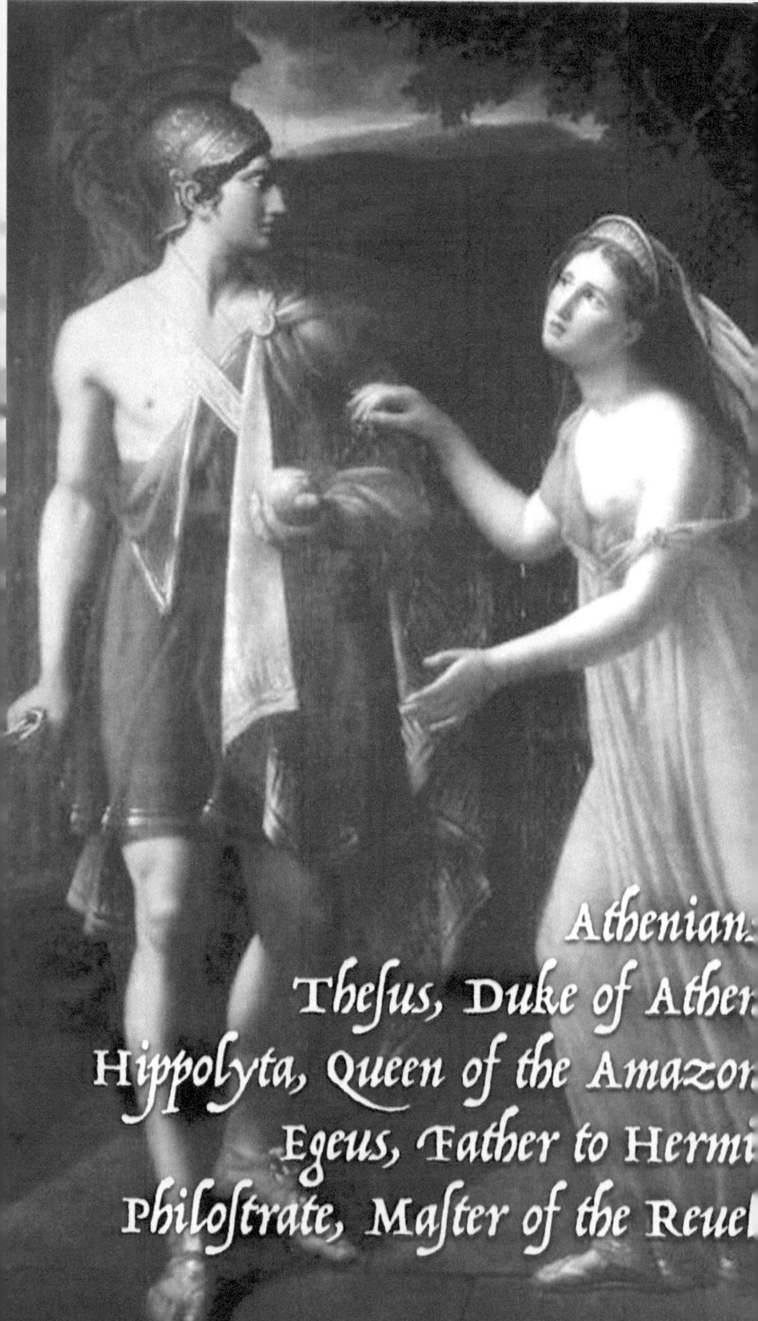

Athenian
Theſus, Duke of Athen
Hippolyta, Queen of the Amazon
Egeus, Father to Hermi
Philoſtrate, Maſter of the Reuel

A Midsommer nights dreame.

As it hath beene sundry times pub-
lickely *acted*, by the *Right honoura*-
ble, the Lord Chamberlaine his
seruants.

Written by William Shakespeare.

¶ Imprinted at London, for *Thomas Fisher*, and are to
be soulde at his shoppe, at the Signe of the White Hart,
in *Fleetestreete*. 1600.

A MIDSOMMER Nights Dreame.

Enter Theſeus, Hippolita, with others.

Theſeus.

Now faire *Hippolita*, our nuptiall houre

Drawes on apace: four happy daies bring in

Another Moone: but oh, me-thinks, how flow

This old Moone wanes: She lingers my deſires

Like to a Step-dam, or a Dowager,

Long withering out a young mans reuenew.

  Hip. Four daies will quickly ſteepe themſelues in nights

Four Daies will quickly dreame away the time:

And then the Moone, like to a ſilver bow,

Now bent in heauen, ſhall behold the night

Of our ſolemnities.

  The. Goe *Philoſtrate,*

Stirre vp the *Athenian* youth to merriments,

Awake the peart and nimble ſpirit of mirth,

Turne

1

A Midſommer Nights Dreame.

Turne melancholy foorth to Funerals :

The pale companion is not for our pompe.

Hippolita, I woo'd thee with my ſword,

And wonne thy loue, doing three injuries:

But I will wed thee in another key,

With pompe, with triumph, and with reuelling.

     Enter Egeus and his daughter Hermia, and Lyſander,

        Helena, and Demetrius.

  Ege. Happy be *Theſeus,* our renowned Duke.

  The. Thanks good *Egeus.* What's the newes with thee?

  Ege. Full of vexation, come I, with complaint

Againſt my childe, my daughter *Hermia.*

      Stand foorth Demetrius.

My noble Lord,

This man hath my conſent to marry her,

      Stand foorth Lyſander.

And my gracious Duke,

This man hath bewitch the boſome of my childe :

Thou, thou, *Lyſander,* thou haſt giuen her rimes,

And interchang'd loue tokens with my childe :

Thou haſt by moone-light at her window ſung,

And ſtrong preuailement in vnhardened youth)

With cunning haſt thou filcht my daughters heart,

Turnd her obedience (which is due to me)

            To

A Midſommer Nights Dreame.

To ſtubborne harſhneſſ. And my gracious Duke,

Be it ſo ſhe will not here before your Grace,

Conſent to marry with *Demetrius,*

I beg the ancient priuilege of *Athens* ;

As ſhe is mine, I may diſpose of her ;

Which ſhall be either to this fentlement,

Or to her death, according to our law,

Immediately prouided in that cafe.

 The. What fay you *Hermia* ? be aduis’d, faire maid,

To you your father ſhold be as a God :

One that compos’d your beauties ; yea and one,

To whom you are but as a form in wax

By him imprinted, and within his power,

To leaue the figure, or disfigure it :

Demetrius is a worthy gentleman.

 Her. So is *Lyſander.*   *The.* In himſelfe he is.

But in this kinde, wanting your fathers voice,

The other muſt be held the worthier.

 Her. I would my father lookt but with my eyes.

 The. Rather your eyes muſt with his judgement looke.

 Her. I do intreate your Grace to pardon me.

I know not by what power I am made bold,

Nor how it may concern my modeſty,

If ſuch a preſence, here to plead my thoughts ;

But

A Midſommer Nights Dreame.

But I beſeech your Grace, that I may know
The worſt that may befall me in this caſe,
If I refuſe to wed *Demetrius.*

    The. Either to die the death, or to abiure
For euer the ſociety of men.
Therefore faire *Hermia,* queſtion your deſires,
Know of your youth, examine well your blood,
Whether (if you yield to your fathers choyce)
You can endure the liuery of a Nunne,
For aye to be in ſhady Cloiſter mew'd
To liue a barren ſister all your life,
Chanting faint hymnes to the colde fruitleſſe Moone.
Thice bleſſed that they maſter ſo their blood,
To vndergo ſuch maiden pilgrimage,
But earthliet happy is the Roſe diſtild,
Then that which withering on the Virgin thorne,
Growed, liues, and dies, in ſingle bleſſedneſſe.

    *Her.*So will I grow, ſo liue, ſo dye, my Lord,
Ere I will yield my virgin Patent vp
Vnto his Lordship, whoſe vnwiſshed yoake
My ſoule conſents not to giue ſouerainty.

    *The.*Take time to pauſe, and by the next new Moone,
The ſealing day betwixt my loue and me,
For euerlaſting bond of fellowſhip :
Vpon that day either prepare to dye,

For

4

A Midſommer Nights Dreame.

For diſobediance to your fathers will,

Or elſe to wed *Demetrius,* as he wold,

Or on *Dianaes* Altar to proteſt,

For ate, auſterity, and ſingle life.

    Dem. Relent ſweete *Hermia,* and *Lyſander,* yield

Thy crazed title to my certaine right.

    Lyſ. You haue her Fathers loue, *Demetrius* :

Let me have *Hermias* : do you marry him.

    Egeus. Scornful *Lyſander,* true, he hath my Loue ;

And what is mine, my loue ſhall render him

And ſhe is mine, and all my right of her

I do eſtate vnto *Demitrius.*

    Lyſan. I am my Lord, as well deriu'd as hee

As well poſſeſt : my loue is more then his :

My fortunes euery way as fairely ranckt

(If not with vantage) as *Demetrius* :

And (which is more then all theſe boaſts can be)

I am belou'd of beauteous *Hermia.*

Why ſhould not I then proſecute my right?

Demetrius, Ile auouch it to his head,

Made loue to *Nedars* daughter, *Helena,*

And won her foule : and ſhe (ſweete Lady) dotes,

Deuoutly dotes, dotes in Idolatry,

Vpon this ſpotted and inconſtant man.

    The. I must confeſſ, that I haue heard ſo much,

And

A Midſommer Nights Dreame.

And with *Demetrius,* thought to haue ſpoke thereof ;

But being ouer full of ſelfe-affaires,

My minde did loſe it. But *Demetrius* come,

And come *Egeus,* you ſhall go with me,

I haue ſome priuate ſchooling for you both.

For you faire *Hermia,* looke you arme your ſelfe,

To fit your fathers will ;

Or elſe the Law of *Athens* yeelds you vp

(Which by no means we may extenuate)

To death, or to a vow of ſingle life.

Come my *Hippolita* ; what cheare my loue?

Demetrius and *Egeus* gow along :

I muſt imploy you in ſome buſineſſe

Againſt our nuptial, and conferre with you

Of ſomething, neerely that concernes your ſelues.

    Ege. With duty and deſire, we follow you.   *Exeunt.*

    Lyſ. How now my loue? Why is your cheeke ſo pale?

How chance the roſes there do faſe ſo faſt?

    Her. Belike for want of raine ; which I could well

Beteeme them, from the tempeſt of my eyes.

    Lyſ, Eigh me ; for ought that I could euer reade,

Could euer heare by tale or hiſtory,

The courſe of trye loue neuer did runne ſmoothe,

But either it was different in bloud ;

    Her. O croſſe ! too high to be inthrald to louc.

Lyſ.

A Midfommer Nights Dreame.

Lyf. Or elfe mifgraffed, in refpect of years ;

Her. O fpight ! too olde to be ingag'd to yong.

Lyf. Or elfe it ftood vpon the choife,

Warre, death, or fickneffe, did lay fiedge to it ;

Making it momentany, as a found ;

Swift as a fhadow ; fhort as any dreame ;

Briefe as the lightening in the collied night,

That (in a fpleene) fnfolds both heauen and earth ;

And ere a man hath power to fay, behold,

The iawes of darkneffe do deuoure it vp :

So quicke bright things come to confufion.

Her. If then Louers haue bin euer croft,

It ftands as an edict in deftiny :

Then let vs teach our trial patience,

Becaufe it is a cuftomary croffe,

As due to loue, as thoughts, and dreames, and fighes,

Wifhes and teares ; poore Fancies followers.

Lyf. A good perfwafion : therefore heare me, *Hermia* :

I have a widow Ant, a dowager,

Of great reuenew, and fhe hath no childe,

From *Athens* is her houfe remote fefen leagues,

And fhe refpects me, as her onely fonne :

There gentle *Hermia*, may I marry thee,

And to that place, the fharpe *Athenian* law

Cannot purfure vs. If thou loueft me, then

Steale

Steale forth thy fathers houſe, to morrow night.

And in the wood, a leagye without the towne

(Where I did meete thee once with *Helena,*

To do obſeruance to a morne of May)

There will I ſtay for thee.

    Her. My good *Lyſanſder,*

If we are to thee, by *Cupids* ſtrongeſt bow,

By his belt arrow, with the golden head,

By the ſimplicity of *Venus* Doues,

By that which knitteth ſoules, and proſpers loue,

And by that fire which burnd the Carthage Queene,

When the falſe Troyan vnder fayle was feene,

By all the vowes that euer men haue broke,

(In number more then euer women ſpoke)

In that ſame place thou haſt appointed me,

To morrow truly will I meete with thee.

    Lyſ. Keepe promiſe loue, looke here comes *Helena.*

Enter Helena.

    Her. God ſpeede faire *Helena,* whither away?

    Hel. Call you me faire ? that faire againe vnſay,

Demetrius loues your faire : O happy faire !

Your eyes are loadſtars, and your tongues ſweet ayre

More tuneable then Larke to Shepheards eare,

When wheate is green, when hauthorne buds appeare,

Sickneſſe is catxhing : O vvere fauour ſo,

Your

A Midſommer Nights Dreame.

Your vvords I catch, faire *Hermia* ere I goe,
My eare ſhold catch your tongues ſweet melody,
Were the vvorld mine, *Demetrius* being bated,
The reſt Ile giue to be to you tranſlated.
 O teach me how you looke, and vvith vvhat art,
You fvvay the motion of *Demetrius* heart.

    Her. I frowne vpon him, yet he loues me ſtill.
    Hel. O that your frowns wold teach my ſmiles ſuch skil
    Her. I giue him curſes, yet he giues me loue.
    Hel. O that my prayers could such affection mooue.
    Her. The more I hate, the more he followes me.
    Hel. The more I loue, the more he hateth me.
    Her. His folly, *Helena* is none of mine.
    Hel. None but your beauty, wold that faul: were mine.
    Her. Take comfort : he no more ſhall ſee my face,
Lyſander and my ſelfe will fly this place.
Before the time I did *Lyſander* ſee,
Seem'd *Athens* like a Paradice to me.
O then, what graces in my Loue do dwell,
That he hath turn'd a heauen into hell.

    Lyſ. Helen, to you our minds we will vnfold,
To morrow night, when *Phœbe* doth behold
Her ſiluer viſage, in the watry glaſſe,
(A time, that louers flights doth ſtill conceale)
Through *Athens* gates, haue we deuiſed to ſteale.

Her.

9

"

A Midſommer Nights Dreame.

Her. And in the woo, where often you and I,

Vpon faint Pimroſe beds, were wont to lye,

Emptyig our boſomes, of their counſell ſweld,

There my *Lyſander,* and my ſelfe ſhall meete,

And thence from *Athens* turne away our eyes

To ſeeke new friends and ſtrange companions.

Farwell ſweete play-fellow, pray thou for vs,

And good lucke grant thee thy *Demetrius.*

Keepe word *Lyſander* we muſt ſtarue or fight.

Exit Hermia.

Lyſ. I will my *Hermia. Helena,* adieu,

As you on him, *Demetrius* dote on you,   *Exit Lyſ.*

Hel. How happy ſome, ore otherſome can be?

Through *Athens* I am thought as faire as ſhe.

But what of that ? *Demetrius* thinks not ſo :

He will not know, what all, but he do know,

And as he erres, doting on *Hermias* eyes ;

So I, admiring his qualities :

Things baſe and vile, holding no quantity,

Loue can transſpoſe to forme and dignity,

Loue looks not the the eyes, but with the minde,

And therefore is wingd *Cupid* painted blinde.

Nor hath loues minde of any judgement taſte :

Wings, and no eyes, figure, vnheedy haſte.

And therefore is loue ſaid to be a childe,

Becauſe

10

A Midſommer Nights Dreame.

Becauſe in choiſe he is oft beguilde,

As waggiſh boyes in game themſelues forſweare ;

So the boy Loue is periur'd euery where.

For ere *Detremius* lookt on *Hermias* eyne,

He haild downe oaths that he was onely mine.

And when his haile, ſome heate from *Hermia* felt,

So he diſſolu'd, and ſhowres of oaths did melt,

I will go tell him of faire *Hermias* flight :

Then to the wood will he, to morrow night

Purſue her ; and for this intelligence,

If I haue thanks, it is a deare expence :

But herein meane I to enrich my paine,

To haue his ſight thither, and back againe.   *Exit.*

Enter Quince the Carpenter, Snug the Ioyner, Bottome the Weauer, Flue the Bellows-mender, Snout the Tinker, & Starue-ling the Taylor.

Quin. Is all our company here ?

Bot. You were beſt to call them generally, man by man, according the ſcrippe.

Quin. Here is the ſcrowle of euery mans name, which is thought fit through all *Athens,* to play in our Enterlude, be-fore the Duke & the Dutches, on his wedding day at night,

Bot. Firſt good *Peter Quince,* ſay what the play treats on : then read the names of the Actors : and ſo grow to a point.

Quin. Marry our plat is the moſt lamentable Comedy,

and

and moſt cruell death of *Tyramus* and *Thisbie*.

Bot. A very good peece of worke, I aſſure you, & a merry. Now good *Peter Quince*, call foorth your Actors by the ſcrowle. Maſters ſpread your ſelues.

Quin. Anſwer as I call you. *Nick Bottom* the Weauer.

Bot. Ready ; name what part I am for, and proceed.

Quin. You *Nick Bottom* are ſet downe for *Pyramus*.

Bot. What is *Pyramus*, a louer, or a tyrant ?

Quin. A louer that kils himſelfe moſt gallant, for loue.

Bot. That will aske ſome teares in the true perfourming of it, if I doe it, let the auidience looke to their eyes : I will moue ſtormes ; I will condole in ſome meaſure. To the reſt yet, my chiefe humour is for a tyrant.   I could play *Ereles* rarely, or a part to teare a Cat in, to make all ſplit the raging Rocks ; a ſhiuering ſhocks ſhall ſhine from farre, & make and marre the fooliſh Fates. This was lofty.   Now name the reſt of the players. This is *Ercles* vaine, a tyrants vaine : a louer is more condoling.

Quin. Francis Flute the Bellowes-mender.

Flu. Here *Peter Quince*.

Quin. You must take *Thisby* on you.

Flu. What is *Thisby* ? a wandering Knight ?

Quin. It is the Lady that *Pyramus* muſt loue.

Fl. Nay faith, let not me play a woman, I haue a beard coming.

Quin.

A Midſommer Nights Dreame.

Quin. That's all one, you ſhal play it in a Maske, and you may ſpeake as ſmall as you will.

Bot. And I may hide my face, let me play *Thisby* to : Ile ſpeake in a monſtrous little voice ; *Thiſne, Thiſne,* ah *Pyramus* my louer deare, thy *Thisby* deare, and Lady deare.

Quin. No no, you muſt play *Pyramus,* & *Flute,* you *Thisby.*

Bot. Well, proceed. *Qu. Robin Starueling* the Tailor.

Star. Heere *Peter Quince.*

Qu. Robin Starueling, you muſt play *Thisbies* mother : *Tom Snowt,* the Tinker.

Snowt. Here *Peter Quince.*

Quin. You, *Pyramus father ; my* ſelfe, *Thisbies* father ; *Snugge* the Ioyner, you the Lyons part : and I hope here is a play fitted.

Snug. Haue you the Lyons part written ? pray you if it be, giue it me, for I am flowe of ſtudy.

Quin. You may do it *extempore,* for it is nothing but roaring.

Bot. Let me play the Lyon too, I will roare, that I will do any mans heart good to heare me. I will roare, that I will make the Duke ſay, Let him roare again, let him roare againe.

Quin. If you ſhould do it too terribly, you would fright the Dutcheſſe and the Ladies, that they would ſhrike, and that were enough to hang vs all.

All.

13

A Midſommer Nights Dreame.

All. That would hang vs euery mothers ſonne.

Bot. I grant you friends, if you ſhould fright the Ladies out of their wits, they would haue no more diſcretion but to hang vs : but I will aggrauate my voice ſo, that I will roare you as gently as any ſucking Doue ; I will roare you and t'were any Nightingale.

Quin. You can play no part but *Piramus*, for *Piramus* is a ſweet fac't man, a proper man as one ſhal ſee in a ſommers day ; a moſt louely gentlemanlike man, therefore you muſt needs play *Piramus.*

Bot. Well, I will vndertake it. What beard were I beſt to play it in ?

Quin. Why, what you will.

Bot. I will diſharge it, in eyther your ſtraw colour beard, your orange tawny beard, your purple in graine beard, or your french crowne colour beard, your perfit yellow.

Quin. Some of your french crownes haue no haire at all ; and then you will play barefac't.   But maſters heere are your oarts, and I am to entreat you, requeſt you, and deſire you, to con them by too morrow night: and meete me in the palace wood, a mile without the towne, by Moone-light, there we will rehearſe: for if we meete in the Citty, we ſhall be dogd with company, and our deuiſes knowne. In the meane time, I will draw a bill of properties, ſuch as our play wants. I pray you faile me not.

Bot.

14

A Midſommer Nights Dreame.

Bot. We will meete, and there we may rehearſe more obſeenely and couragiouſly. Take paines, be perfit, adieu.

Quin. At the Dukes oke we meete.

Bot. Enough, hold or cut bow-ſtrings.　　　　　　*Exeunt.*

Enter a fairy at one doore, and Robin good-fellow

at another.

Robin. How now ſpirit, whether wander you?

Fai. Ouer hill, ouer dale, through buſh, through brier,

Ouer parke, ouer pale, through flood, through fire,

I do wander euery where, ſwifter then the Moons ſphere ;

And I ſerue the Fairy Queene, to dew her orbes vpon the

The cowſlips tall, her penſioners be,　　　　　　(greene.

In their gold coats, ſpots you ſee,

Thoſe be Rubies, Fairy fauours,

In thoſe freckles, liue their fauors,

I muſt goe ſeeke ſome dew drops here,

And hang a pearle in euery cowſlips eare.

Farwell thou Lov of ſpirits, Ile be gone,

Our Queene and all her Elues come here anon,

　Rob. The King doth keepe his Reuels here to night,

Take heed the Queene come not within his ſight,

For *Oberon* is paſſing fell and wrath,

Becauſe that ſhe, as her attendant, hath

A louely boy stolen from an Indian king,

She neuer had ſo ſweete a changeling,

　　　　　　　　　　　　　　　　　And

A Midſommer Nights Dreame.

And iealous *Oberon* would haue the childe,
Knight of his traine, to tace the loued boy,
Crownes him with flowers, and makes him all her joy.
And now they neuer meete in groue, or greene,
By fountaine cleere, or ſpangled ſtarlight ſheene,
But they do ſquare, that all their Elues for feare
Creepe into acorne cups, and hide them there.

   Fai. Either I miſtake your ſhape and making quite,
Or elſe you are that ſhrewd and knauish ſprit,
Call'd *Robin good-fellow.* Are you not hee,
That frights the maidens of the Villagree,
Skim milke, and ſometimes labour in the querne,
And bootleſſe make the breathleſſe huſwife cherne,
And ſometime make the drinke to beare no barme,
Miſ-leade night-wanderers, laughing at their harme,
Thoſe that hobgoblin call you, and ſweete Puck,
You do their worke, and they ſhall haue good lucke.
Are not you he?   (the night,

   Rob. Thou ſpeak'ſt aright ; I am that merry wanderer of
I ieaſt to *Oberon,* and make him ſmile,
When I a fat and beane-fed horſe beguile ;
Neighing in likeneſſe of a filly foale,
And ſometime lurke I in a goſſips bole,
In very likeneſſe of a roſted crab,
And when ſhe drinkes, againſt her lips I bob,

                             And

A Midſommer Nights Dreame.

And on her withered dewlop poure the ale.

The wiſeſt Aunt telling the ſaddest tale,

Sometime for three foote ſtoole, miſtaketh me,

Then flip I from her bum, downe topples ſhe,

And tailour cryes, and fals into a coffe,

And then the whole Quire hold their hips, and loffe,

And waxen in their mirth, and neeze, and ſweare,

A merrier houre was neuer waſted there.

But roome Fairy, here comes *Oberon.*

    Fai. And here my miſtreſſe : would that he were gone,

        Enter the King of Fairies at one doore with his traine,

            And the Queene at another with hers.

    Ob. Ill met by moone-light, proud *Tytania.*

    Queene. What, iealous *Oberon?* Fairy, skip hence,

I haue forſworne his bed and company.

    Ob. Tarry raſh wanton ; am not I thy Lord?

    Qu. Then I muſt be thy Lady : but I know

When thou haſt ſtollen awat from Fairy Land,

And in the ſhape of *Corin,* fat all day,

Playing on pipes of corne, and verſing loue,

To amorous *Phillida.* Why art thou here

Come from the fartheſt ſteepe of *India?*

But that forſooth the bouncing *Amazon,*

Your buskind miſtreſſe, and your warrior loue,

To *Theſeus* muſt be wedded ; and you come,

To

A Midſommer Nights Dreame.

To giſe their bed ioy and proſperity.

    Ob. How canſt thou thus for ſhame, *Tytania,*
Glance at my credire, with *Hippolita?*
Knowing I know thy loue to *Theſeus.*
Didſt not thou leade him through the glimmering night,
From *Perigenia,* whom he reuiſhed?
And make him with faire Eagles breake his faith
With *Ariadne,* and *Antiopa?*

    Queene. Theſe are the forgeries of iealouſie,
And neuer ſince the middle Sommers ſpring,
Met we on hill, in dale, forreſt or mead,
By paued fountaine, or by ruſhy brooke,
Or in the beached margent of the ſea,
To dance our ringlets to the whiſtling winde,
But with thy brawles thou haſt diſturbd our ſport.
Therefore the windes, pyping to vs in vaine,
As in reuenge, haue ſuckt vp from the ſea,
Contagious fogs ; which falling in the Land,
Hath euery pelting riuer made ſo proud,
That they haue ouer-borne their Continents.
The Oxe hath therefore ſtretcht his yoke in vaine,
The ploughman loſt his ſweat, and the greene Corne
Hath rotted, ere his youth attaind a beard:
The fold ſtands empty, in the drowned field,
And Crowes are fatted with the murrion floke,

The

A Midſommer Nights Dreame.

The nine mens Morris is fild vp with mud,
And the quient Mazes in the wanton greene,
For lacke of tread, are vndiſtinguiſhable.
The humane mortals want their winter heere,
No night is now with hymme or carroll bleſt ;
Therefore the Moone (the gouerneſſe of floods)
Pale in her anger, waſhes all the aire ;
That Rheumaticke diſeaſes do abound.
And through this diſtemperature, we ſee
The ſeaſons alter ; hoared headed froſts
Fall in the freſh lap of the crimſon Roſe,
And on old *Hyems* chinne and Icie crowne,
An odorous Chapler of ſweete Sommer buds
Is as in mockery ſet. The Spring, the Sommer,
The childing Autumne, angry Winter change
Their wonted Liueries, and the mazed world,
By their increaſe, no knows not which is which ;
And this ſame progeny of euils,
Comes from our debate, from our diſſention,
We are their parents and originall.

 Oberon. Do you amend it then, it lyes in you,
Why ſhould *Titania* croſſe her *Oberon*?
I do but beg a little changeling boy,
To be my Henchman.

 Queene. Set your heart at reſt,

The

19

A Midſommer Nights Dreame.

The Fairy land buies not the childe of me,
His mother was a Votreſſe of my order,
And in the ſpiced *Indian* aire, by night
Full often hath ſhe goſſipt by my ſide,
And ſat with me on *Neptunes* yellow ſands,
Marking th'embarked traders on the flood,
When we haue laught to ſee the ſailes conceiue,
And grow big bellied with the wanton winde,
Which ſhe with pretty and with ſwimming gate,
Following (her wombe then rich with my young ſquire)
Would imitate and faile vpon the Land,
To fetch me trifles, and returne againe,
As from a voyage, rich with merchandize.
But ſhe being mortall, of that boy did dye,
And for her ſake do I rare vp her boy,
And for her fake I will not part with him.

    Ob. How long within this wood intend you ſlay?

    Queen. Perchance till after *Theſeus* wedding day.
If you will patiently dance in our Round,
And ſee our Moone-light reuels, go with vs ;
If not, ſhun me and I will ſpare your haunts.

    Ob. Giue me that boy, and I will ſo with thee.

    Qu. Not for thy Fairie Kingdome. Fairies away :
We ſhall chide downe right, if I longer ſtay.   *Exeunt.*

    Ob. Well, go thy way : thou ſhalt not from the groue,

Till

A Midſommer Nights Dreame.

Till I torment thee for this injury.

My gentile *Puck* come hither ; thou remembreſt

Since once I ſat vpon a promontory,

And heard a Meare-maide on a Dolphins backe,

Vttering ſuch dulbet and harmonious breath,

That the rude ſea grew ciuill at her ſong,

And certaine ſtarres ſhot madlt from their Spheares,

To heare the Sea-maids muſicke.

 Puc. I remember.

 Og. That very time I ſay (but thou couldſt not)

Flying between the colde Moone and the earth,

Cupid all arm'd ; a certaine aime he tooke

At a daire Veſtall, throned by Weſt,

And loos'd his loue-ſhaft ſmartly from his bow,

As it ſhould pierce a hundred thouſand hearts,

But I might ſee young *Cupids* firey ſhaft

Quencht in the chaſte beames of the watry Moone ;

And the imperiall Votreſſe paſſed on,

In maiden meditation, fancy free.

Yet markt I where the volt of *Cupud* fel.

It fell vpon a little weſterne flower ;

Before, milke-white ; now purple with loues wound,

And maidens call it, Loue in idelneſſe.

Fetch me that flower ; the hearb I ſhew'd thee once,

The idyce of it, on ſleeping eye-lids laide,

Will

"

A Midfommer Nights Dreame.

Will make or man or woman madly dote

Vpon the nexr liue creature that it fees.

Featch me this hearbe, and be thou here againe,

Ere the *Leviathan* can fwim a league.

    Pu. Ile put a girdle about the earth, in forty minutes.

    Oberon. Hauing once this iuyce,

Ile watch *Titania*, whence fhe is afleepe,

And drop the liquor of it in her eyes:

The next thing when fhe waking looks vpon,

(Be it on Lyon, Beare, or Wolfe, or Bull,

On medling Monket, or on bufie Ape)

She fhall purfue it, with the foule of loue.

And ere I take this charme off from her fight,

(As I can take it with another hearbe)

Ile make her render vp her Page to me,

But who comes heere? I am inuifible,

And I will ouer-heare their conference.

         Enter Demetrius, Helena following him.

    Deme. I loue thee not, therefore purfue me not,

Where is *Lyfander*, and faire *Hermia?*

The one Ile ftay, the other ftayeth me.

Thou toldft me they were ftolne vnto this wood ;

And here I am, and wood within this wood,

Becaufe I cannot meete my *Hermia.*

Hence, get thee gone, and follow me no more.

                                         Hel.

A Midſommer Nights Dreame.

Hel. You draw me, you hard-hearted Adamant,
But yet you draw not Iron, for my heart
Is true as ſteele. Leaue you your power to draw,
And I ſhall haue no power to follow you.

Deme. Do I entice you ? do I ſpeake you faire
Or rather do I not in plaineſt truth,
Tell you I do not, not I cannot loue you?

Hel. And euen for that do I loue thee the more
I am your ſpaniell, and *Demetrius,*
The more you beate me, I will fawne on you.
Vſe me but as your ſpaniell; ſpurne me, ſtrike me,
Neglect me, loſe me ; only giue me leaue
(Vnworthy as I am) to follow you.
What worſer place can I beg in your loue,
(And yet a place of high reſpect with me)
Then to be vſed as you vſe your dog.

Dem. Tempt not too much the hatred of my ſpirit, for I
am ſicke when I do look on thee.

Hel. And I am ſicke when I looke not on you.

Deme. You do impeach your modeſty too much,
To leaue the Cilty, and commit your ſelfe
Into the hands of one that loues you not,
To truſt the opportunity of night,
And the ill counſell of a deſert place,
With the rich worth of your virginity.

Hel.

23

A Midſommer Nights Dreame.

Hel. Your virtue is my priuiledge : for that
It is not night when I do ſee your face.
Therefore I thinke I am not in the night,
Nor doth this wood lacke worlds of company,
For you in my reſpect are all the world.
Then how can it be ſaid I am alone,
When all the world is here to looke on me?

Dem. He run from thee, and hide me in the breakes,
And leaue thee to the mercy of wilde Beaſts.

Hel. The wildeſt hath not ſuch a heart as you ;
Runne when you will, the ſtory ſhall be chaung'd :
Apollo flyes, and *Daphna* holds the chaſe ;
The Doue purſues the Griffen, the milde Hinde
Makes ſpeed to catch the Tygre. Bootleſſe ſspeede,
When cowardiſe purſues, and valor flyes.

Demet. I will not ſtay thy queſtions, let me go ;
Or if thou follow me, do not beleeue,
But I ſhall do thee miſchiefe in the wood.

Hel. I, in the temple, in the Towne, and Field
You do me miſchiefe. Fye *Demetrius,*
Your wrongs do ſet a ſcandall on my ſex :
We cannot fight for loue, as men mat do ;
We ſhould be woo'd, and were not made to wooe.
Ile follow thee and make a heauen of hell,
To dye vpon the hand I loue ſo well.   *Exit.*

C

A Midſommer Nights Dreame.

Ob. Fare thee well Nymph, ere he do leaue this groue,

Thou ſhalt flye him, and he ſhall ſeeke thy loue.

Haſt thou the flower there? Welcome wanderer.

Enter Pucke.

Puck. I, there it is.

Ob. I pray thee giue it me.

I know a banke where the wilde time blowes,

Where Oxtflips and the nodding Violet growes,

Quite ouervanoped with luſhious woodbine,

With ſweete musk roſes, and with Eglantine ;

There ſleepes *Tytania,* ſometime of the night,

Luld in theſe flowers, with dances and delight :

And there the ſnake throwes her enammeld skinne,

Weed wide enough to rap a Fairy in.

And with the juyce of this, Ile ſtrake her eyes,

And make her full of hatefull fantaſies.

Take thou ſome of it, and ſeeke through this groue;

A ſweete *Athenian* Lady is in loue

With a diſdainefull youth : anoint his eyes,

But do it when the nect thing he eſpies,

May be the Lady. Thou ſhalt know the man,

By the *Athenian* farments he hath on.

Effect it vvith ſome care, that he may prooue

More fond on her, then ſhe vpon her loue ;

And looke thou meete me ere the firſt Crocke crow.

Pu.

A Midsommer Nights Dreame.

Pu. Feare not my Lord, your feruant fhall do fo. *Exeunt.*

Enter Queene of Fairies, with her traine.

Queen. Come, now a Roundell, and a Fairy fong ;

Then for the third part of a minute hence,

Some to kill cankers in the muske rofe buds,

Some warre with Reremife, for their leathern wings,

To make my final Elues coates, and fome keepe backe

The clamorous Owle, that nightly hootes and wonders

At our queint fpirits : Sing me now afleepe,

Then to your offices, and let me reft.

Fairies fing.

You fpotted fnakes with double toungue,

Thorny Hedgehogges be not feene,

Newts and blinde wormes do no wrong

Come not neere our Fairy queene.

Philomele with melody,

Sing in our fweett Lullaby,

Lulla, lulla, lullaby, lulla, lulla, lullaby,

Neuer harme, nor fpell, nor charme,

Come our louely Lady nye,

So good night with Lullaby.

I. Fairy. Weaning Spiders come not heere,

Hence you long legd Spinders, hence :

Beetles, blacke approch not neere ;

Worme nor Snayle do no offence.

Philimele

26

A Midſommer Nights Dreame.

Philimele with meoldy, &c.

   2. *Fai. Hence away, now all is well ;*

One aloofe, ſtand Centinell.

Enter Oberon.

  Ob. What thou feeſt when thou doſt wake,

Do it for thy thy trye loue take :

Loue and languiſh for his fake.

Be it Ounce, or Catte, or Beare,

Pard, or Boare with briſtled haire,

In thy eye that fhall appeare,

When thou wak'ſt, it is thy deare,

Wake when fome vile thing is neere.

Enter Lyſander and Hermia.

  Lyſ. Faire loue, you faint with wandring in the woods,

And to fpeake troth I haue forgot our way :

Wee'l reſt vs *Hermia,* if you thinke it good,

And tarry for the comfort of the day.

  Her. Be it fo *Lyſander* ; finde you out a bed,

For I vpon this banke will reſt my head.

  Lyſ. One turffe fhall ferue as pillow for vs both,

One heart, one bed, two bofomes, and one troth.

  Her. Nay good *Lyſander* for the fake my deare

Lue further off yet, do not lue fo neere.

  Lyſ. O take the fence fweete, of my innocence,

Loue takes the meaning, in loues conference,

I

27

A Midſommer Nights Dreame.

I meane that my heart vnto yours is knit,
So that but one heart we can make of it.
Two boſomes interchained with an oath,
So then two boſomes, and a ſingle troth.
Then by your ſide, no bed-roome me deny,
For lying ſo, *Hermia*, I do not lye.

    Her. Lyſander riddles very prettily ;
Now much beſhrew my manners and my pride,
If *Heria* meant to ſay, *Lyſander* lied.
But gentle friend, for loue and courteſie
Lie further off, in humane modeſty,
Such ſeparation, as may well be ſaid,
Becomes a virtuous batchellor, and a maide,
So farre be diſtant, and good night ſweet friend ;
Thy loue nere alter till thy ſweete life ende.

    Lyſ. Amen, amen, to that faire praier, ſay I,
And then end life, when I end loualty :
Heere is my bed, ſleepe giue thee all his reſt.

    Her. With halfe that wiſh, the wiſhers eyes be preſt.

Enter Pucke.

    Puck. Through the Forreſt haue I gone,
But *Athenian* I finde I none,
On whoſe eies I might approue
This dlowers dorce in ſtirring loue.
Night and ſilence : who is heere ?

VVeedes

28

A Midſommer Nights Dreame.

VVeedes of *Athens* he doth weare :

This is he (my maſter ſaid)

Deſpiſed the *Athenian* maide :

And heere the maiden ſleeping found,

On the danke and dirty ground.

Pretty foule, ſhe durſt not lye

Neere this lack-loue, this kill-curteſie.

Churle, vpon thy eyes I throw

All the power this charme doth owe :

VVhen tho wak'ſt, let loue forbid

Sleepe his feate, on thy eye-lid.

So awake when I am gone :

For I muſt now to *Oberon*.   *Exit.*

> *Enter Demetrius and Helna running.*

   Hel. Stay though thou kill me, ſweete *Demetrius.*

   De. I charge thee hence, and do not haunt me thus.

   Hel. O wilt thou darkling leaue me? Do not ſo.

   De. Stay on thy perill, I alone will goe.

   Hel. O I am out of breath, in this fond chaſe,

The more my praier, the leſſer is my grace.

Happy is *Hermiu,* whereſocre ſhe lies ;

For ſhe hath bleſſed and attractiue eyes.

How came her eyes ſo bright ? Not with ſalt teares.

If ſo, my eies are oftner waſht then hers.

No, no, I am vgly as a Beare ;

For

A Midſommer Nights Dreame.

For beaſts that meete me, runne away for feare,
Therefore no maruaile, though *Demetrius*
Do as a monſter, flie my preſence thus.
What wicked and diſſembling glaſſe of mine,
Made me compare with *Hermias* ſphery eyne ?
But who is here, *Lyſander* on the grouud ?
Dead or aſleepe? I ſee no blood, no wound,
Lyſander, if you liue, good ſir awake.

    Lyſ. And run through fire I will for thy ſweet ſake.
Tranſparant *Helena,* nature ſhewes arte,
That through thy boſome makes me ſee thy heart.
Where is *Demetrius*? Oh how fit a word
Is that vile name, to periſh on my ſword!

    Hel. Do not ſay ſo *Lyſander,* ſay not ſo :
What though he loue your *Hermia*? No, I do repent
The tedius minutes I with her haue ſpent.
Not *Hermia,* but *Helena* now I loue ;
Who will not change a Rauen for a Doue?
The will of man is by his reaſon ſwai'd :
And reaſon ſaies you are the worthier maid.
Things growing are not ripe vntill their ſeaſon ;
So I being young, till now ripe not to reaſon,
And touhing now the point of humane skill,
Reaſon becomes the Marſhall to my will,
And leads me to your eyes, where I orelooke

Loues

30

A Midsommer Nights Dreame.

Loues ftories, written in Loues richeft booke.

    Hel. Wherefore was I to this keene mockery borne?

When at your hands did I deferue this fcorne?

Ift not enough, ift not enough, young man,

That I did neuer, no nor neuer can,

Deferue a fweete looke from *Demetrius*_eye,

But you muft flout my infufficency?

Good troth you do me wrong (good-footh you do)

In fuch difdainfull manner, me to wooe.

But fare you well ; perforce I muft confeffe,

I thought you Lord of more true gentleneffe.

Oh, that a Lady of one man refvs'd,

Should of another therefore be abus'd   *Exit.*

    Lyf. She sees not *Hermia* : *Hermia*, fleepe thou there,

And neuer maift thou come *Lyfander* neere ;

For as a furfet of the fweeteft things

The deepeft loathing to the ftomacke brings;

Or as the herefies that men do leaue,

Are hated moft of thofe they did decieue :

So thou, my furfet, and my herefie,

Of all be hated ; but the moft of me ;

And all my powers addreffe your loue and might,

To honour *Helen*, and to be her Knight.   *Exit.*

    Her. Helpe me *Lyfander*, helpe me ; do thy beft

To plucke this crawling ferpent from my breft.

                              Aye

A Midſommer Nights Dreame.

Aye me, for pitty ; what dreame was here ?

Lyſander looke, how I do quake with feare :

Me-thought a ſerpent eate my heart away,

And you fat ſmiling at his cruell prey.

Lyſander, what remoou'd? *Lyſander*, Lord,

What, out of hearing, gone? No found, no word?

Alake where are you? ſpeake and if you heare ;

Speake of all loues ; I ſwound almoſt with feare,

No, then I well perceiue you are not nye,

Eyther death or you ile finde immediately.   *Exit.*

Enter the Clownes.

Bot. Are we all met ?

Quin. Pat, pat, are heres a maruailous convenient place for our rehearſall. This greene plot ſhall be our ſtage, this hauthorne brake our trying houſe, and we will doe it in ac-tion, as we will do it before the Duke.

Bot. Peter quince?

Peter. What ſaiſt thou, bully *Bottome* ?

Bot. There are things in this Comedy of *Piramus_*and *Thisby*, that will neuer pleaſe. First, *Piramus* muſt draw a ſword to kill himſelfe ; which the Ladyes cannot abide.

How anſwer you that ?

Snout. Berlaken, a parlous feare.

Star. I beeeue we muſt leaye the killing out, when all is done.

Bot.

32

A Midſommer Nights Dreame.

Bot. Not a whit, I haue a deuice to make all well. Write me a Prologue, and let the Prolouge feeme to fay, wee will do not harme with our fwords, and that *Pyramus* is not kild indeed : and for the more better affurance, tell them that I *Piramus* am not *Piramus,* but *Bottome* the Weauer ; this will put them out of feare.

Quin. Well, we will haue fuch a Prologue, and it fhall be written in eight and fixe.

Bot. No, make it two more, let it be written in eight & eight.

Snout. Will not the Ladies by afeard of the Lyon?

Star. I feare it, I promife you.

Bot. Mafters, you ought to confider with your felfe, to bring in (God fhield vs) a Lyon among Ladies, is a moft. *dreadfull thing.* For there is not a more fearefull wilde fowle that your Lyon liuing: and we ought to looke to it.

Snout. Therefore another Prologue muft tell he is not a Lyon.

Bot. Nay, you muft name his name, and halfe his face muft be feene through the Lyons necke, and hee himfelfe muft fpeake through, faying this, or to the fame deffect ; Ladies, or faire Ladies, I would wifh you, or I would re-queft you, or I would entreat you not to feare, not to trem-ble : my life for yours. If you thinke I come hether as a Ly-on, it were pitty of my life. No, *I* am no fuch thing, *I* am a

man

A Midſommer Nights Dreame.

man as other men are ; and there indeed let him name his name, and tell them plainly his is *Snug* the ioyner.

Quin. Well, it ſhall be ſo ; but there is two hard things, that is, to bring the Moone-light into a chamber : for you know, *Piramus* and *Thisby* meete by Moone-light.

Sn. Doth the Moon ſhine that night we play our play?

Bottom. A Calender, a Calender, looke in the Almanack, finde out Moone-ſhine that night.

Bot. Why then may you leaue a caſement of the great Chamber window (where we play) open, and the Moone may ſhine in at the caſement.

Quin. I, or elſe one muſt come in with a buſh or thorns,& a lanthorne, and ſay he comes to disfigure, or to preſent the perſon of Moon-ſhine.   Then there is another thing, we muſt haue a wall in the great Chamber ; for *Piramus* and *Thisby* (faies the ſtory) did talke through the chinke of a wall.

Sn. You can neuer bring in a wall. What ſay you *Bottome* ?

Bot. Some man or other muſt preſent wall, and let him haue ſome plaſter, or ſome lome, or ſome rough caſt about him, to ſignifie wall ; or let him fold his fingers thus; and through that cranny, ſhall *Piramus* and *Thisby* whiſper.

Quin. If that may be, then all is well. Come, ſit downe e-uery mothers ſonne, and rehearſe your parts. *Piramus*, you begin ; when you haue ſpoken you ſpeech, enter into that

Brake

A Midſommer Nights Dreame.

Brake, and ſo euery one according to his cue.

Enter Robin.

Rob. What hempen home-ſpuns haue we ſwaggring here,

So neere the Cradle of the Fairy Queene?

What, a play toward? Ile be an auditor,

An actor too perhaps, if I ſee cauſe.

Quin. Speake *Piramus*, *Thisby* ſtand forth.

Pir. Thisby, the flowers of odious fauors ſweete.

Quin. Odours, odorous,

Pir. Odours fauors ſweete,

So hath thy breath, my deareſt *Thisby* deare.

But harke, a voyce : ſtay thou but heere a while,

And by and by I will to thee appeare.   *Exit.*

Quin. A ſtranger *Piramus*, then ere plaid here.)

Thiſ. Muſt I ſpeake now?

Pet. I marry muſt you. For you muſt vnderstand he goes

But to ſee a noyſe that he heard, and is to come againe.

Thſ. Most radiant *Piramus, moſt* Lilly white of hue,

Of colour like the red roſe on triumphant bryer,

Moſt brisky Iuuenall, and eke moſt louely Iew,

As true as trueſt horſe, that yet would neuer tyrc,

Ile meete thee *Piramus*, at *Ninnies* toombe.

Pet. Ninus toombe man: why you muſt not ſpeake that

yet ; that you anſwer to *Piramus* : you ſpeake all your part

at once, cues and al. *Piramus* enter, your cue is paſtl it is

neuer

35

A Midſommer Nights Dreame.

neuer tyre.

Thyſ. O, as true as trueſt horſe, that yet would neuer tyre.

Pir. If I were faire, *Thisby* I were onely thine.

Pet. O monſtrous, O ſtrange. We are haunted ; pray maſters, flye maſters, helpe.

Rob. Ile follow you, Ile leade you about a Round,

Through bogge, through buſh, through brake, through

Sometimes a horſe Ile be, ſometime a hound,   (bryer

A hogge, a headleſſ beare, ſometime a fire,

And neigh, and barke and grunt, at euery turne.   *Exit.*

Bot. Why do they run away ? This is a knauery of them

To make me afeard.   *Enter Snowt.*

Sn. O *Bottom,* thou art chang'd ; what do I ſee on thee?

Bot. What do you ſee ? you ſee and aſſe head of your own.
Do you

Enter Peter quince.

Per. Bleſſe thee *Bottome,* bleſſe thee ; thou art tranſlated.

Exit.

Bot. I ſee their knauery ; this is to make an aſſe of me, to
fright me if they could ; but I will not ſtir from this place,
do what they can. I will walke vp and downe heere, and I
will ſing that they ſhall heare I am not afraid.

The Woofell cocke, ſo blacke of hew,

With Orange tawny bill,

The Throſtle, with his note ſo true,

The

A Midfommer Nights Dreame.

The Wren with little quill.

 Tytania. What Angell wakes me from my flowry bed ?

 Bot. The Finch, the Sparrow, and the Larke,

The plainfong Cuckow gray ;

Whofe note full many a man doth marke,

And dares not anfwer, nay.

For indeed, who would fet his wit to fo foolifh a bird?

Who would giue a bird the lye, though he cry Cuckow, ne-

uer fo?

 Tyta. I pray thee gentle mortall, fing againe,

Mine eare is much enamored of thy note ;

On the firft view to fay, to fweare I loue thee,

So is mine eye enthralled to thy fhape,

And thy faire vertues force (perforce) doth moue me,

 Bot. Me-thinks miftreffe, you fhould haue little reafon

for that : and yet to fay the truth, reafon and loue keepe lit-

tle company together, no adayes. The more the pitty, that

fome honeft neighbours will not make them friends. Nay

I can gleeke vpon occafion.

 Tyta. Thou art as wife, as thou art beautifull.

 Bot. No fo neither : but If I had wit enough to get out

Of this wood, I haue enough to ferue mine owne turne.

 Tyta. Out of this wood, do not defire to goe,

Thou fhalt remaine here, whether thou wilt or no.

I am a fpirit of no common rate :

The

A Midſommer Nights Dreame.

The Sommer ſtill doth tend vpon my ſtate,
And I do loue thee ; therefore go with me,
Ile giue thee Fairies to attend on thee ;
And they ſhall fetch thee Iewels from the deepe,
And ſint, while thou on preſſed flowers doſt ſleepe
And I will purge thy mortall groſſeneſſe ſo
That thou ſhalt like an ayry ſpirit go.

Peaſe-bloſſome, Cobweb, Moth, and Muſtard-ſeed

Enter foure Fairies.

Fai. Ready ; and *I*, and *I*. Where ſhall we go ?

Tita. Be kinde and courteous to this Gentleman,
Hop in his walkes, and gambole in his eies,
Feede him with Apricocks, and Dewberries,
With purple Grapes, greene Figs, and Mulberrires,
The honie-bags ſteale from the humble Bees,
And for night tapers, crop their waxen thighes,
And light them at the fiery Glow-wormes eies,
To haue my loue to bed, and to ariſe
And plucke the wings from painted butterflies,
To fanne the Moone-beames from his ſleeping eyes,
Nod to him Elues, and do him curtſies.

I. *Fai.* Haile mortall, haile.

2. *Fai.* Haile.

3. *Fai.* Haile.

Bot. I cry your worſhips mercy hartily ; I beſeech your

worſhips

38

A Midſommer Nights Dreame.

worſhips name.

Cob. Cobweb.

Bot. I ſhall deſpire you of more acquaintance, good Maſter *Cobweb* : if *I* cut my finger, *I* ſhall make bold with you.
Your name honeſt gentleman?

Peaſ. Peaſe-bloſſome.

Bot. I pray you commend me to miſtreſſe *Squaſh*, your
Mother, and to maſter *Peaſcod* your Father. Good maſter
Peaſe-bloſſome, *I* ſhall deſire you of more acquaintance to,
Your name I beſeech you ſir?

Muſ. Muſtard ſeede.

Bot. Good maſter *Muſtard ſeed*, I know your patience
well : that fame cowardly gyant-like Oxe-beefe hath de-
uoured many a gentleman of your houſe. I promiſe you,
your kindred hath made me eyes water ere now. I deſire
you more acquaintance, food Maſter *Muſtardſeed*

Tita. Come waite vpon him, leade him to my bower,
The Moone me-thinks, looks with a warey eie,
And when ſhe weeps, weepe euery little flower,
Lamenting some enforced chastity.
Tye vp my louers tongue, bring him ſilently.　　*Exit.*
Enter King of Faires, and Robin good-fellow,

*Ob.*I wonder if *Titania* be awak't ;
Then what it was that next came in her eye,
Which ſhe muſt dote on, in extremity,

Here

39

A Midſommer Nights Dreame.

Here comes my meſſenger : how now mad ſpirit,

What night-rule now about this haunted groue?

   Puck. My miſtriſſe with a monſter is in loue,

Neere to her close and conſecrated bower,

While ſhe was in her dull and ſleeping hower,

A crew of patches, rude Mechanicals,

That worke for bread, vpon *Athenian* ſtalles,

Were met together to rehearſe a play,

Intended for great *Theſeus* nuptiall day :

The ſhalloweſt thick-skin of that barren ſort,

Who *Piramus* preſented, in their ſport,

Forſooke his Scene, and entred in a brake,

When I did him at this aduantage take,

An Aſſes nole I fixed on his head.

Anon his *Thisbie* must be anſwered,

And forth my Minnock comes : when they him ſpy,

As wilde-geeſe, that the creeping Fowler eye,

Or ruſſed pated choughes, many in ſort

(Rising and cawing at the guns report)

Seuer themſelues, and madly ſweepe the sky:

So at his ſight, away his fellowes flye,

And at our ſtampe, here ore and ore one falles;

He murther cryes, and helpe from *Athens* cals.

Their ſenſe thus weake, loſt with their feares thus ſtrong,

Made

A Midſommer Nights Dreame.

Made ſenſleſſe things begin to do them wrong.

For briars and thornes at their apparell ſnatch,

Some ſleeues, ſome hats, from yeelders all things catch,

I led them on in this diſtracted feare,

And left ſweete *Piramus* tranſlated there:

When in that moment (ſo it came to paſſe)

Tytania waked, and ſtraightaway lou'd an aſſe.

    Ob. This falles out better then I could deuiſe :

But haſt thou yet lacht the *Athenians* eyes,

With the loue iuyve, as I did bid thee do ?

    Rob. I tooke him ſleeping (that is finiſht to)

And the *Athenian* woman by his ſide,

That when he wak't, of force ſhe muſt be cyde.

Enter Demetrius and Hermia.

    Ob. Stand cloſe, this is the ſame *Athenian.*

    Rob. This is the woman, but not this the man.

    Deme. O why rebuke you him that loues you ſo ?

Lay breath ſo bitter on your bitter foe.

    Her. Now I but chide, but I ſhould vſe thee worſe.

For thou haſt ſlaine *Lyſander* in his ſleepe,   (to

Being ore ſhooes in bloud, plunge in tho deepe, and kill me

The Sunne was no ſo true vnto the day,

As he to me. Would he haſe ſtollen away,

From ſleeping *Hermia* ? Ile beleeue as ſoone

This whole earth may be bor'd, and that the Moone

May

41

A Midſommer Nights Dreame.

May through the Center creepe, and ſo diſpleaſe
Her brothers noonetide, with th' *Antipodes*.
It cannot be but thou haſt murdred him,
So ſhould a murderer looke, ſo dead, ſo grim.

 Dem. So ſhould the murdered looke,& ſo ſhould I,
Pierſt through the heart with your ſtearne cruelty :
Yet you the murderer looke as bright, as cleare,
As yonder *Venus* in her glimmering ſpheare.

 Her. VVhat's this to my *Lyſander* ? where is he ?
Ah good *Demetrius*, wilt thou giue him me ?

 Dem. Ide rather giue his carkaſſe to my hounds.

 Her. Out dog, out curre, thou driu'ſt me paſt the bonds
Of maidens patience. Hast thou ſlaine him then?
Henceforth be neuer numbered among men.
Oh, once tell true, euen for my ſake,
Durſt thou haue lookt vpon him, being awake ?
And haſt thou kild him ſleeping ? O braue touch :
Could not a worme, and Affer do ſo much ?
An Adder did it. For with doubler tongue
Then thing (thou ſerprent) neuer Affer ſtung.

 Dem. You ſpend your paſſion on a miſprinz'd mood,
I am not guilty of *Lſanders* bloud :
Nor is he dead, for ought that I can tell.

 Her. I pray thee tell me then, that he is well.

 Dem. And if I could, what ſhould I get therefore ?

Her.

A Midſommer Nights Dreame.

Her. A priuiledge, neuer to ſee me more,

And from thy hated preſence part I, ſee me no more,

Whether he be dead or no.   *Exit.*

    Dem. There is no following her in this fierce vaine,

Heere therefore for a while I will remaine.

So ſorrowes heauineſſe doth heauier grow.

For debt that bankrout ſlip doth ſorrow owe,

Which now in ſome flight meaſure it will pay,

If for his tender heere I make ſome ſtay.   *Lie downe.*

    Ob. What haſt thou done ? Thou haſt miſtaken quite,

And laide the loſe iuyce on ſome true loſes ſight :

Of thy miſpriſion, muſt perforce enſue

Some true loue turn'd, and not a falſe turnd true.

    Rob. Then fate ore-rules, that one man holding troth,

A million faile, confounding oath on oath.

    Ob. About the wood, goe ſwifter then the winde,

And *Helena* of *Athens* looke thou ſinde.

All fancy ſicke ſhe is, and pale of cheere,

With ſighs of loue, that coſts the freſh bloud deare.

By ſome illuſion ſee thou bring her heere,

Ile charme his eies, againſt ſhe do appeare.

    Robin. I go, I go, looke how I goe,

Swifter then arrow from the *Tartars* bowe.   *Exit.*

    Ob. Flower of this purple die,

Hit with *Cupids* archery,

Sinke

A Midſommer Nights Dreame.

Sinke in apple of his eye,

When his loue he doth eſpy,

Let her ſhine as gloriouſly

As the *Venus* of the sky,

When thou wak'ſt, if ſhe be by,

Beg of her for remedy.

Enter Pucke.

Puc,ze. Captaine of our Fairy band,

Helena is heere at hand,

And the youth, miſtooke by me,

Pleading for a Louers fee.

Shall we their fond Pageant ſee ?

Lord, what fooles theſe mortals be !

Ob. Stand aſide : the noyſe they make,

Will cauſe *Demetrius* to awake.

Puc. Then will two at once wooe one,

That muſt needs be ſport alone :

And thoſe things do beſt pleaſe me,

That befall prepoſterouſly.

Enter Lyſander and Helena.

Lyſ. Why ſhould you think that I ſhould wooe in ſcorn ?

Scorne and deriſion neuer come in teares :

Looke when I vow I weepe ; and vowes ſo borne,

In their natiuity all truth appeares.

How can theſe things in me, ſeeme ſcorne to you ?

Bearing

A Midſommer Nights Dreame.

Bearing the badge of faith to proue them true.

 Hel. You do adſuance your cunning more and more,

When truth kils truth, O diueliſh holy fray !

Theſe vowes are *Hermias.* Will you giue her ore ?

Weigh oath with oath, and you will nothing weigh.

Your vowes to her, and me (put in two ſcales)

Will euen weigh, and both as light as tales.

 Lyſ. I had no judgement, when to her I ſwore.

 Hel. Nor none in my minde, now you guie her ore.

 Lyſ. Demetrius loues her, and he loues not you.

 Deme. O *Helen*, goddleſſe, nymph, perfect, diuine,

To what, my loue, ſhall I compare thine eine !

Chriſtall is muddy, O how ripe in ſhowe,

Thy lips, thoſe kiſſing cherries, temnpting grow !

That pure congealed white, high *Taurus* ſnow,

Fan'd with the Eaſterne winde, turns to a crow,

When thou holdſt vp thy hand, O let me kiſſe

This Princeſſe of pure white, this ſeale of bliſſe.

 Hell. O ſpight ! o hell ! I ſee you all are bent

To ſet againſt me, for your merriment.

If you were ciuill, and knew curteſie,

Can you not hate me, as I know you do,

But you muſt ioyne in foules to mackme me too ?

If you were men, as men you are in ſhow,

You would not vſe a gentle Lady ſo ;

To

A Midſommer Nights Dreame.

To vow, and ſweare, and ſuperpraiſe my parts,
When I am ſure you hate me with your hearts,
You both are Riuals, and loue *Hermia* ;
And now both Riuals, to mocke *Helena.*
A trim exploit, a manly enterprize,
To coniure teares vp in a poore maides eyes,
With your deriſion, none of noble ſort,
Would ſo offend a virgine, and exrort
A poore ſoules patience, all to make you ſport,

   Lyſan. You are vnkind *Demetrius* ; be not ſo.
For you loue *Hermia* ; this you know I know ;
And heere with all good will, with all my heart,
In *Hermia* loue I yield you vp my part ;
And yours of *Helena,* to me bequeath,
Whom I do loue, and will do to my death.

   Hel. Neuer did mockers waſte more idle breath.

   Deme. Lyſander, keepe thy *Hermia,* I will none :
If ere I lou'd her, all that loue is gone.
Winke each at other, hold the ſweete ieaſt vp :
This ſport well carried, ſhall be chronicled.
If you haue any pitty, grace, or manners,
You would not make ſuch and argument.
But faryewell, tis partly mine owne fault,
VVhich death or abſence ſoone ſhall remedy.

   Lyſ. Stay gentle *Helena,* heare my excuſe,

My

A Midſommer Nights Dreame.

My loue, my life, my foule, faire *Helena.*

    Hel. O excellent !

    Her. Sweete, do not fcorne her fo.

    Dem. If fhe cannot entreate, I can compell.

    Lys. Thou canft compell, no more than fhe entreate.

Thy threats haue no more ftrength then her weake praife.

Helen, I loue thee, by my life I doe ;

I fweare by that which I lofe for thee,

To proue him falfe, that faies I loue thee not.

    Dem. I fay, I loue thee more then he can do.

    Lyſ. If thou fay fo, with fraw and proue it to.

    Dem. Quick, come.

    Her. Lyſander, whereto tends all this ?

    Lyſ. A way, you *Ethiope.*

    Dem. No, no, hee'l feeme to breake loofe ;

Take on as you would follow,

But yet come not : you are a tame man, go.

    Lyſ. Hang off thou cat, thou bur ; vile thing let loofe,

Or I will fhake thee from me like a ferpent.

    Her. VVhy are you growne fo rude ?

VVhat change is this, fweete Loue ?

    Lyſ, Thy loue ? out Tartar, out ;

Out loathed medicine ; ô hated poifon hence.

    Her. Do you not ieaft ?

    Hel. Yes footh, and fo do you.

Lyſ.

A Midſommer Nights Dreame.

Lyſ. *Demetrius*, I will keepe my word with thee,

Dem. I would I had your bond : for I perceiue,

A weake bond holds you ; Ile not truſt your word.

Lyſ. VVhat, ſhould I hurt her, ſtrike her, kill her

dead ?

Although I hate her, Ile not harme her ſo.

Her. VVhat ? can you do me greater harme then hate ?

Hate me, wherefore ? O me, what newes my Loue ?

Am not I *Hermia* ? Are not you *Lyſander* ?

I am as faire now, as I was ere while.

Since night you lou'd me ; yet ſince night you left me.

VVhy then you left me (ô the gods forbid)

In earneſt, ſhall I ſay ?

Lyſ. I, by my life ;

And neuer did deſire to ſee thee more.

Therefore be our of gope, of queſtion, of doubt ;

Be certaine ; nothing truer ; tis no ieaſt,

That I do hate thee, and loue *Helena.*

Her. O me, you iuggler, you canker bloſſome,

You theeſe of loue ; what, haue you come by night,

And ſtolen me loues heart from him ?

Hel. Fine ifaith.

Haue you no modeſty, no maiden ſhame,

No touch of baſhfulneſſe ? VVhat, will you teare

Impatient anſwers from my gentle tongue ?

Fie,

A Midſommer Nights Dreame.

Fie, fie, you counterfet, you puppet, you.

 Her. Puppet ? why ſo ? I, that way goes the game.
Now I perceiue that ſhe hath made compare
Betweene our ſtatures, ſhe hath vrg'd her height,
And with her perſonage, her tall perſonage,
Her height (forſooth), ſhe hath prebuild with him.
And are you growne ſo high in his eſteeme,
Becauſe I am ſo dwarfiſh and ſo low ?
How low am I, thou painted May-pole ? Speake,
How low am I ? I am not yet ſo low.
But that my nailes can reach vnto thine eyes.

 Hel. I pray you though you mocke me, gentlemen,
Let her not hurt me ; I was neuer curſt :
I haue no gift at all in ſhrewiſhneſſe:
I am a right maid for my cowardize ;
Let her no ſtrike me : you perhaps may thinke,
Becauſe ſhe is ſomething lower then my ſelfe,
That I can match her.

 Her. Lower ? harke again.

 Het. Good *Hermia,* do not be ſo bitter with me,
I euermore did loue you *Hermia,*
Did euer keepe your counſels, neuer wronged you,
Saue that in loue vnto *Demetrius,*
I told him of your ſtealth vnto this wood.
He followed you, for loue I followed him,

            But

A Midſommer Nights Dreame.

But he hath chid me hence, and threatned me

To ſtrike me, ſpurne me, nat ro kill me to ;

And now, ſo you will let me quier goe,

To *Athens* will I beare my folly backe,

And follow you no further. Let me go.

You ſee how ſimple, and how fond I am.

    Her. Why get you gone : who iſt that hinders you ?

    Hel. A fooliſh heart, that I leaue heere behinde.

    Her. VVhat, with *Lyſander* ?

    Hel. VVith *Demetrius.*

    Lyſ. Be not afraid, ſhe ſhall not, though you take her part.

    Hel. O when ſhee's angry, ſhe is keene and ſhrewd,

She was a vixen when ſhe went to ſchoole,

And though ſhe be but little, ſhe is fierce.

    Her. Little againe ? Nothing but low and little ?

VVhy will you ſuffer her to flout me thus ?

Let me come to her.

    Lyſ. Get you gone you dwarfe,

You *minimus,* of hindring knot graſſe made,

You bead, you acorne.

    Dem. You are too officious,

In her behalf that ſcornes your ſeruices.

Let her alone, ſpeake not of *Helena,*

Take not her part. For if thou doſt intend

Neuer ſo little ſhew of loue to her,

Thou

A Midſommer Nights Dreame.

Thou ſhalt abie it.

    Lyſ. Now ſhe holds me not,

Now follow if thou dar'ſt, to try whoſe right,

Of thine or mine, is moſt in *Helena.*   (*Exit.*

    Dem. Follow ? Nay, Ile go with thee cheeke by iowle.

    Her. You Miſtreſſe, all this coyle is long of you.

Nay, goe not backe.

    Hel. I will not truſt you I,

Not londer ſtay in your curſt company.

Your hands than mine, are quicker for a fray,

My legs are longer though to runne away.

    Her. I am amaz'd, and know not what to ſay.   *Exeunt.*

    Ob. This is thy negligence, ſtill thou miſtak'ſt,

Or elſe commit'ſt thy knaueries wilfully.

    Puck. Beleeue me, King of ſhaddowes, I miſtooke.

Did not you tell me, I ſhould know the man,

By the *Athenian* garments he hath on ?

And ſo farre blameleſſe proues my enterprize,

That I haue nointed an Athenians eyes,

And ſo farre am I glad, it ſo did ſort,

As this their iangling I eſteeme a ſport.

    Ob. Thou ſeeſt theſe Louers ſeeke a place to fight,

Hie therefore *Robin,* ouercaſt the night,

The ſtarry Welkin couer thou anon,

With drooping fogge as blacke as *Acheron,*

                            And

A Midſommer Nights Dreame.

And leade theſe teſty Riuals ſo aſtray,
As one come not within anothers way.
Like to *Lyſander,* ſometime frame thy toungue,
Then ſtirre *Demetrius* vp with bitter wrong ;
And ſometime raile thou like *Demetrius* ;
And from each other looke thou leade them thus,
Till ore their broweds, death-counterfeiting, ſleepe
With leaden ledgs, and Batty wings doth creepe ;
Then cruſh this hearbe into *Lyſanders* eie,
Whoſe liquor hath this vertuous property,
To take from thence all error, with his might,
And makle his eie bals rolle with wonted fight.
When they next wake, all this deriſion
Shall ſeeme a dreame, and fruitleſſe viſion,
And backe to *Athens* ſhall the Louers wend
With league, whoſe date till death ſhall neuer end.
Whiles I in this affaire do thee apply,
Ile to my Queene, and neg her *Indian* boy ;
And then I will her charmed eie releaſe
From monſters view, and all things ſhall be peace.

   Puck. My Fairie Lord, this muſt be done with haſte,
For night ſwift Dragons cut the Clouds full faſt,
And yonfer ſhines *Auroras* harbinger ;
At whoſe approach, Ghoſts wandring heere and there,
Troope home to Church-yards ; damned ſpirits all,

That

A Midſommer Nights Dreame.

That in croſſe waies and flouds haue buriall,

Already to their wormy beds are gone ;

For feare leaſt day ſhould looke their ſhames vpon,

They wilfully themſelues exile from light,

And muſt for aie conſort with blacke browd night.

    Ob. But we are ſpirits of another ſort :

I, with the mornings loue haue oft made ſport,

And like a Forreſter, the grouse may tread,

Euem till the Eaſterne gate all fiery red,

Opening on *Neptune*, with faire bleſſed beames,

Turnes into yellow gold, his falt greene ſtreames.

But not withſtanding haſte, make no delay,

We mat effect this buſineſſe, yet ere day.

    Puck. Vp and downe, vp and downe, I will leade them vp

& downe : I am feard in field and towne. *Goblin*, lead them

Vp and downe : here comes one.   *Enter Lyſander.*

    Lyſ. Where art thou, proud *Demetrius* ? Speak thou now.

    Rob. Here villaine, drawne and ready. Where art thou ?

    Lyſ. I will be with thee ſtraight.

    Rob. Follow me then to plainer ground.

        Enter Demetrius.

Deme. Lyſander, ſpeake againe ;

Though runaway, thou coward, art thou fled ?

Speake in ſome buſh. Where doſt thou hide thy head ?

    Rob. Thou coward, art thou bragging to the ſtars,

                    Telling

A Midſommer Nights Dreame.

Telling the buſhes that thou look'ſt for warres,
And wilt not come ? Come recreant, come thou childe,
Ile whip thee with a rod. He is defil'd
That drawes a ſword on thee.

    Deme. Yea, art thou there ?

   Ro. Follow my voice, wee'l try no manhood here. *Exeunt.*

    Lyſ, He goes before me, and ſtill dares me on,
When I come where he calles, the hee's gone.
The villaine is much lighter heel'd then I ;
I followed faſt, but fater he did flie ;
That fallen am I in darke vneuen way,
And here will reſt me. Come thou gentle day :
For if but once thou ſhew me thy gray light,
Ile finde *Demetrius,* and reuenge this ſpight.

      Robin and Demetrius.

   Rob. Ho, ho, ho ; coward, why com'ſt thou not ?

   Deme. Abide me, if thou dar'ſt. For well I wot,
Thou runſt before me, ſhifting euery place,
And dar'ſt not ſtand, nor looke me in the face.
Where art thou ?

   Rob. Come hither, I am here.

   De. Nay then thou mockſt me ; thou ſhalt buy this deare,
If euer I thy face by day-light ſee.
Now goe thy way : faintneſſe conſtraineth me,
To meaure out my length on this cold bed,

                             By

A Midſommer Nights Dreame.

By daies approch looke to be viſted.

Enter Helena.

  Hel. O weary night, ô long and tedious night,

Abate thy hours, ſhine comforts from the eaſt,

That I may backe to *Athens* by day-light,

From theſe that my poore company deteſt ;

And ſleepe that ſometimes ſhuts vp ſorrowes eie,

Steale me a while from mine owne company.   *Sleepe.*

  Rob. Yet but three ? Come one more,

Two of both kindes make vp foure.

Here ſhe comes, curſt and ſad,

Cupid is a knauish lad,   *Enter Hermia.*

Thus to make poore females mad.

  Her. Neuer ſo weary, neuer ſo in woe,

Bedabbled with the dew, and torne with briars,

I can no further crawle, no further goe ;

My legs can keepe no pace with my deſires.

Here will I reſt me till the breake of day,

Heauens ſhield *Lyſander*, if they meane a fray.

  Rob. On the ground ſleepe found,

Ile apply your eye gentle louer, remedy,

VVhen thou wak'ſt, thou tak'ſt

True delight in the ſight of thy former Ladies eie,

And the Country Prouerbe knowne,

That euery man ſhould take his owne,

In

55 "

A Midſommer Nights Dreame.

In your waking ſhall be ſhowne.

Iacke ſhall haue *Iill*, nought ſhall go ill,

The man ſhall haue his Mare againe, and all ſhall be well.

> *Enter Queene of Fairies, and Clowne, and Fairies, and the*
>
> *King behinde them.*

Tita. Come ſit thee downe vpon this flowry bed,

While I thy amiable cheekes do coy,

And ſticke muske roſes in thy ſleeke ſmoothe head,

And kiſſe thy faire large eares, my gentle ioy.

Clowne. Where's *Peaſe-bloſſome* ?

Peaſ. Ready.

Clowne. Scratch my head, *Peaſe-bloſſome.* Wher's Mounſieur *Cobweb* ?   *Cob.* Ready.

Clo. Mounſieur *Cobweb*, good Mounſieur get your
weapons in your hand, and kill me a red hipt bumble-
bee, on the top of a thiſtle ; and good Monſieur bring
me the hony bad. Doe not fret your ſelfe too much in
the action, Mounſieur ; and good Mounſieur haue a
care the hony bag. Breake not, I would be loth to haue
you ouerflowne with a hony-bag ſigniour. Where's
Mounſieur *Muſtardſeed* ?

Muſ. Ready.

Clo. Giue me your neafe, Mounſieur *Muſtardſeed*

Muſ. What's your wil ?

Clo. Nothing good Mounſieur, but to helpe Caualery

Cobweb

56

A Midſommer Nights Dreame.

Cobweb to ſcratch. I muſt to the Barbers Mounſieur, for
me-thinkes I am maruailous hairy about the face. And I
am ſuch a tender aſſe, if my haire do but tickle me, I muſt-
ſcratch.

    Tita. What, wilt thou heare ſome ſome muſick, my ſweet
loue ?

    Clowne. I haue a reaſonable good eare in muſicke. Let vs.
Haue the tongs and the bones.

    Tita. Or ſay ſweete Loue, what thou deſireſt to eate.

    Clow. Truly a pecke of prouender ; I could mounch your
Good dry Oates. Me-thinkes I haue a great deſire to a bot-
tle of hay : good hay, ſweete hay hath no fellow.

    Tita. I haue a venturous Fairy,
That ſhall ſeeke the ſquirrels hoard,
And fetch thee new Nuts.

    Clo. I had rather haue a handful or two of dried peaſe.
But I pray you let none of your people ſtir me, I haue an ex-
poſition of ſleepe come vpon me.

    Tyta. Sleepe thou, and I will winde thee in my armes,
Fairies be gone, and be alwaies away.
So doth the woodbine, the ſweete Honifuckle,
Gently entwiſt l the female Iuy ſo
Enrings the barky fingers of the Elme.
O how I loue thee ! how I dote on thee !

        Enter Robin goodfellow.

                                         Ob.

A Midſommer Nights Dreame.

Ob. Welcome good *Robin* : ſeeſt thou this ſweet ſight?
Her dotage now I do begin to pitty.
For meeting her of late behind the wood,
Seeking ſweete fauors for this hatefull foole,
I did vpbraid her, and fall out with her.
For ſhe his hairy temples then had rounded,
With coronet of freſh and fragrant flowers.
And that ſame dew which ſomtime on the buds,
VVas wont to ſwell like round and orient pearles ;
Stood now within the pretty flouriers eies,
Like teares that did their owne diſgrace bewaile.
When I had at my pleaſure taunted her,
And ſhe in milde tearmes begd my patience,
I then did aske of her, her changeling childe,
Which ſtraight ſhe gaue me, and her Fairy ſent
To beare him to my Bower in Fairy Land.
And now I haue the boy, I will vndoe
This hatefull imperfection of her eies.
And gentle *Pucke*, take this transformed ſcalpe,
From off the head of this *Athenian* ſwaine ;
That he awaking when the other do,
May all to *Athens* backe againe repaire,
And thinke no more of this nights accidents,
But as the firſt I will releaſe the Fairy Queene.

Be

A Midſommer Nights Dreame.

Be as thou waſt wont to be ;

See as thou waſt wont to ſee.

Dians bud, or Cupids flower,

Hath ſuch force and bleſſed power.

Now my *Titania* wake you, my ſweete Queene.

    Tita. My *Oberon*, what viſions haue I ſeene !

Me-thought I was enamored of an Aſſe.

    Ob. There lies your loue.

    Tita. How came theſe things to paſſe ?

Oh, how mine eies doth loathe this viſage now !

    Ob. Silence a while. *Robin* take of this head ;

Titania, muſicke call, and ſtrike more dead

Then common ſleepe ; of all theſe, fine the ſenſe.

    Tita. Muſicke, ho muſicke, ſuch as charmeth ſleepe.

    Rob. When thou wak'ſt, with thine owne fooles eies peep.

    Ob. Sound muſick ; come my Queen, take hands with me

And rocke the ground whereon theſe ſleepers be.

Now thou and I are new in amity,

And will to morrow midnight, ſolemnly

Dance in Duke *Theſeus* houſe triumphantly,

And bleſſe it to all faire poſterity.

There ſhall the paires of faithfull Louers be

VVedded, with *Theſeus*, all in iollity.

    Rob. Fairy King, attend and marke,

I do heare the morning Larke.

Ob.

A Midſommer Nights Dreame.

Ob. Then my Queene in ſilence ſad,

Trip we after the nights ſhade ;

VVe the Globe can compaſſe ſoone,

Swifter then the wandring Moone.

   Tita. Come my Lord, and in our flight,

Tell me how it came this night,

That I ſleeping heere was found,

VVith theſe mortals on the ground.   *Exeunt*

   Enter Theſeus and all his traine.   *Winde hornes*

   Theſ. Goe one of you, finde out the Forreſter,

For now our obſeruation is perform'd ;

And ſince we haue the vaward of the day,

My Loue ſhall heare the muſicke of my hounds.

Vncouple in the VVeſterne valley, let them go ;

Diſpatch I ſay, and finſe the Forreſter.

VVe will faire Queene, vp to the Mountaines top,

And marke the muſicall confuſion

Of hounds and echo in coniunction.

   Hip. I was with *Hercules* and *Cadmus* once,

When in a wood of *Creete* they bayed the Beare

With hounds of *Sparta*; neuer did I heare

Such gallant chiding. For beſides the grouse,

The skies, the fountaines, euery region neere,

Seeme all one mutuall cry. I neuer heard

So muſicall a diſcord, ſuch ſweete thunder.

            Theſ.

A Midſommer Nights Dreame.

Theſ. My hounds are bred out of the *Spartan* kinde,

So flew'd, ſo ſanded, and their heads are hung

With eares that ſweepe away the morning dew,

Crooke kneed, and dew-lapt, like *Theſſalian* Buls,

Slow in purſuite, but matcht in mouth like bels,

Each vnder each. A cry more tuneable

Was neuer hollowd to, nor cheer'd with horne,

In *Creete*, in *Sparta*, nor in *Theſſaly* ;

Iudge when you heare. But ſoft, with nimphs are theſe ?

Egeus. My Lord, this is my daughter heere aſleepe,

And this *Lyſander*, this *Demetrius* is,

This *Helena*, olde *Nedars Helena*,

I wonder of this being heere together.

The. No doubt they roſe vp early, to obſerue

The right of May ; and hearing our intent,

Came heere in grace of our ſolemnity.

But ſpeake *Egeus*, is not this the day

That *Hermia* ſhould giue anſwer of her choyſe ?

Egeus. It is, my Lord.

Th. Go bid the huntſmen wake them with their hornes.

Shout within, they all ſturt up. Winde hornes.

Theſ. Good morrow friends : Saint *Valentine* is paſt,

Begin theſe wood birds to couple now ?

Lyſ. Pardon, my Lord.

Theſ. I pray you all ſtand vp.

I

A Midſommer Nights Dreame.

I know you two are Riuall enemies.
How comes this gentle concord in the world,
That hatred is ſo farre from ialouſie,
To ſleepe by hate, and feare no enmity.

    Lyſ. My Lord, I ſhall reply amazedly,
Halfe ſleepe, halfe waking. But as yet, I ſweare,
I cannot truly ſay how I came here.
But as I thinke (for truly would I ſpeake)
And now I do bethink me, ſo it is ;
I came with *Hermia* hither. Our intent
Was to be gone from *Athens*, where we might be
Without the perill of the *Athenian* Law.

    Ege. Enough, enough my Lord : you haue enough ;
I beg the Law, the Law, vpon his head :
They would haue ſtolne away, they would, *Demetrius*,
Thereby to haue defeated you and me :
You of your wife, and me of my conſent ;
Of my conſent, that ſhe ſhould be your wife.

    Dem. My Lord, faire *Helen* told me of their ſtealth,
Of this their purpoſe hither, to this wood,
And I in fury hither followed them ;
Faire *Helena*, in fancy followed me.
But my good Lord, I wot not by what power
(But by ſome power it is) my loue
To *Hermia* (melted as the ſnow)

Seemes

A Midſommer Nights Dreame.

Seemes to me now as the remembrance of and idle gaude,

Which in my childehood I did dote vpon :

And all the faith, the virtue of my heart,

The obiect and the pleaſure of mine eie,

Is onely *Helena.* To her, my Lord,

Was I bethroth'd, ere I ſee *Hermia,*

But like a ſickneſſe, did I loathe this food,

But as in health, come to my natural taſte,

Now do I wiſh it, loue it, long for it,

And will for euermore be true to it.

    Theſ. Faire Louers, you are fortunately met ;

Of this diſcourſe, we will heare more anon.

Egeus, I will ouerbeare your will ;

For in the Temple, by and by with vs,

Theſe couples ſhall eternally be knit.

And for the morning now is ſomething worne,

Our purpos'd hunting ſhall be ſet aſide.

Away, with vs to *Athens* ; three and three,

Wee'l hold a feaſt in great ſolemnity.

Come *Hippolita.*   *Exit.*

    Deme. Theſe things ſeeme ſmall and vndiſtinguiſhable,

Like farre off mountains turned into Clouds.

    Her. Me-thingks I ſee theſe things with parted eie,

When euery thing ſeemes double.

    Hel. So me-thinkes :

And

A Midſommer Nights Dreame.

And I haue found *Demetrius,* like a iewell,

Mine owne, and not mine owne.

   Dem. Are you ſure

That we are awake? It ſeems to me,

That yet we ſleepe, we dreame. Do not you thinke,

The Duke was heere, and bid vs follow him ?

   Her. Yea, and my Father.

   Hel. And *Hippolita.*

   Lyſ. And he bid vs follow to the Temple.

   Dem. Why then we are awake ; let's follow him, and by

The way let vs recount our dreames.   *Exit.*

   Clo. When my cue comes, call me, and I will anſwer.

My next is, moſt faire *Piramus.* Hey ho. *Peter Quince* ? *Flute*

the bellowes-mender ? *Snout* the tinker? *Starueling* : Gods my

life ! Stolne hence, and left me aſleepe : I haue had a moſt

rare viſion. I haue had a dreame, paſt the wit of man, to ſay,

what dreame it was. Man is but an Aſſe, if he go about to ex-

pound this dreame. Me-thought I was, there is no man can

tell what. Me-thought I was, and me-thought I had. But man

is but patcht a foole, if he will offer to ſay, what me-thought

I had. The eie of man hath not heard, the eare of man hath

not ſeene, mans hand is not able to taſte, his toungue to con-

ceiue, nor his heart to report, what my dream was.

I will get *Peter Quince* to write a Ballet of this dream,

It ſhall be call'd *Bottomes Dreame,* becauſe it hath no

botome ;

A Midſommer Nights Dreame.

botome ; and I will ſing it in the latter end of a play, before
the Duke. Peraduenture, to make it the more gracious, I
ſhall ſing it at her death.   *Exit.*

Enter Quince, Flute, Thiſbie, and the rabble.

Quin. Haue you ſent to *Bottomes* houſe ? Is he come home
yet ?

Flute. He cannot be heard of. Out of doubt hee is tranſ-
ported.

Thiſ. If he come not, then the play is mard. It foes not
forward, doth it ?

Quin. It is not poſſible : you haue not a man in all *Athens,*
able to diſcharge *Piramus* but he.

Thiſ. No, he hath ſimply the beſt wit of any handy-craft
man in *Athens.*

Quin. Yea, and the beſt perſon too, and he is a very Para-
mour, for a ſweete voyce.

Thiſ. You muſt ſay, Paragon. A Paramount is (God bleſſe
vs) a thing of nought.

Enter Snug the Ioyner.

Snug. Maſters, the Duke is comming from the Temple,
And there is two or three Lords and Ladies more married.
If our ſport had gone forward, we had all beene made men.

Thiſ. O ſweete bully *Bottome* : thus hath he loſt ſixpence
a day, during his life ; he could not haue ſcaped ſixpence a
day.

A Midſommer Nights Dreame.

day.   And the duke had not giuen him sixpence a day for
playing *Piramus,* Ile be hang'd. He would haue deſerued it.
Sixpence a day in *Piramus,* or nothing.

Enter Bottome.

Bot. Where are theſe Lads ? Where are theſe hearts ?

Quin. Bottome, ô moſt courageous day! O moſt happy
houre!

Bot. Maſters, I am to diſcourſe wonders ; but aske
mee not what. For if I tell you, I am not true *Athenian.* I
will tel you euery thing right as it fell out.

Quin. Let vs heare, ſweete *Bottome.*

Bot. Not a word of me : all that I will tell you, is, that
the Duke hath dined. Get yor apparel together, good ſtrings
to your beards, new ribbands to your pumps, meete preſently
at the Palace, euerie man looke ore his part : for the ſhort
and the long is, our play is preferd. In any caſe let *Thiſby*
haue cleane linen : and let not him that plaies the Lion,
paire his nailed, for the ſhall hand out for the Lions clawes.
And moſt deare Actors, eate no Onions, nor Garlicke ; for we
are to vtter ſweete breath, and I do not doubt but to heare
them ſay, it is a ſweete Comedy. No more words : away, go
away.

Enter Theſeus, Hippolita, and Philoſtrate.

Hip. Tis ſtrange my *Theſeus,* that theſe louers ſpeake of.

The. More ſtrange then true. I neuer mat beleeue

Theſe

A Midfommer Nights Dreame.

Thefe anticke fables, nor thefe Fairy toies,
Louers and mad men haue fuch feething braines,
Such fhaping fhantafies, that apprehend more
Then coole reafon euer comprehends.
The Lunaticke, the Louer, and the Poet,
Are of imagination all compact.
One fees more diuels then vafte hell can hold ;
That is the mad man. The Louer, all as franticke,
Sees *Helens* beauty in a brow of *Egipt*.
The Poets eie in a fine frenzy rolling, doth glance
From heauen to earth, from earth to heauen.
And as imagination bodies forth the forms of things
Vnkowne ; the Poets pen turns them to fhapes,
And giues to airy nothing, a locall habitation,
And a name. Such trickes hath ftrong imagination,
That if it would but apprehend fome ioy,
It comprehends fome bringer of that ioy.
Or in the night, imagining fome feare,
How eafie is a bufh fuppos'd a Beare ?
 Hip. But all the ftory of the night told ouer,
And all their minds transfigur'd fo together,
More witneffeth than fancies images,
And growes to fomething of great conftancy ;
But howfoeuer, ftrange and admirable.
 Enter louers : Lyfander, Demetrius, Hermia, and Helena.

Thef.

A Midſommer Nights Dreame.

Theſ, Here come the louers, full of ioy and mirth :
Ioy, gentle friends, ioy and freſh daies
Of loue accompany your hearts.

Lyſ. More then to vs, waite in your roiall walkes, your
boord, your bed.

Theſ. Come now, what maskes, what dances ſhall wee
      haue,
To weare away this long age of three hours,
Betweene or after ſupper, and bed-time ?
Where is our vſuall manager of mirth ?
What Reuels are in hand ? Is there no play,
To eaſe the anguish of a torturing houre ?
Call *Philoſtrate.*

Philo. Heere mighty *Theſeus.*

Theſ. Say, what abridgment haue you for this euening ?
What maske, what muſicke ? how ſhall we beguile
The lazie time, if not with ſome delight ?

Phil. There is a briefe, how many ſports are rife.
Make choiſe of which your Highneſſe will ſee firſt.

Theſ. The battell with the *Centaurs* to be ſung
By an *Athenian* Eunuch, to the Harpe.
Wee'l none of that. That I haue tolde my Loue,
In glory of my kinſman *Hercules.*
The riot of the tipſie *Bachanals,*
Tearing the *Thracian* finger, in their rage ?

That

A Midſommer Nights Dreame.

That is an olde deuice ; and it was plaid,
When I from *Thebes* came laſt a Conqueror.
The thrice three Muſes, mourning for the death
Of learning, late deceaſt in beggery.
That is ſome *Satire* keene and criticall,
Not ſorting with a nuptiall ceremony.
A tedious briefe Scene of young *Piramus*,
And his Loue *Thiſby* ; very tragicall mirth ?
Merry and tragicall ? Tedious and briefe ? That is hot Ice,
And wondrous ſtrange Snow. How ſhall we finde the con-
cord of this diſcord ?

 Philo. A play there is, my Lord, ſome ten words long,
Which is a briefe, a I haue knowne a play ;
But by ten words, my Lord, it is too long ;
Which makes it tedious. For in all the play,
There is not one word apt, one plaier fitted.
And tragicall, my noble Lord, it is : for *Piramus*
Therein doth kill himſelfe. Which when I ſaw
Rehearſt, I muſt confeſſe, made mine eies water ;
But more merry teares the paſſion of loud laughter
Neuer ſhed.

 Theſ. What are they that do play it ?

 Philo. Hard handed men, that worke in *Athens* here,
Which neuer labour'd in their minds till now ;
And now haue toyled their vnbreathed memories,

With

69

A Midſommer Nights Dreame.

With this ſame play, againſt your nuptiall.

    Theſ. And we will heare it.

    Phi. No, my noble Lord, it is not for you. I haue heard
It ouer, and it is nothing, nothing in the world ;
Vnleſſe you can finde ſport in their intents,
Extremely ſtretcht, and cond with cruell paine,
To do you ſeruice.

    Theſ. I will heare that play. For neuer any thing
Can be amiſſe, when ſimpleneſſe and duty tender it.
Goe bring them in, and take your places, Ladies.

    Hip. I loue not to ſee wretchedneſſe orecharged ;
And duety in his ſeruive periſhing.

    Theſ. Why gentle ſweete, you ſhall ſee no ſuch thing.

    Hip. He ſaies, they can do nothing in this kinde.

    The. The kinder we, to giue them thanks for nothing.
Our ſport ſhall be, to take what they miſtake :
And what poore duty cannot do, noble reſpect
Takes it in might, not merit.
Where I haue come, great Clearkes haue purpoſed
To greete me with premeditated welcomes ;
Where I haue ſeene them ſhiuer and looke pale,
Make periods in the midſt of ſentences,
Throttle their practiz'd accent in their feares,
And in concluſion, dumbly haue broke off,
Not paying me a welcome. Truſt me ſweete,

Out

70

A Midſommer Nights Dreame.

Out of this ſilence yet, I pickt a welcome :

And in the modeſty of fearefull duty,

I read as much, as from the ratling tongue

Of ſaucy and audacious eloquence.

Loue therefore, and tongue-tide ſimplicity,

In leaſt, ſpeake moſt, to my capacity.

    Philo. So pleaſe your Grace, the Prologue is addreſt.

    Duke. Let him approach.

Enter the Prologue.

    Pro. If we offend, it is with our good will.

That you ſhould thinke, we come not to offend,

But with good will. To ſhew our ſimple skill,

That is the true beginning of our end.

Conſider then, we come but in deſpight.

VVe do not come, as minding to content you,

Our true intent is, All for yor delight,

VVe are not heere. That you ſhould here repent you,

The Actors are at hand ; and by their ſhow,

You ſhall know all, that you are like to know.

    Theſ. This fellow doth not ſtand vpon points.

    Lyſ. He hath rid his Prologue, like a rough Colt : hee

Lknowes not the ſtop. A good morall my Lord. It is not

enough to ſpeake, but to ſpeake true.

    Hip. Indeed, he hath plaid on this Prologue, like a childe

on a Recorder, a ſound, but not in gouernment.

Theſ.

71

A Midſommer Nights Dreame.

Theſ. His ſpeech was like a tangled chaine ; nothing im-
paired, but all diſordered. Who is next ?

Enter Pyramus and Thisby, Wall, Moone-ſhine, and Lyon.

Prologue. Gentles, perchance you wonder at this ſhow, but
wonder on, till truth make all things plaine.

This man is *Piramus*, if you would know ;

This beautious Lady, *Thisby* is certaine.

This man with lyme and roughcraft, doth preſent

Wall, that vile wall, which did theſe louers ſunder :

And through wals chinke (poore ſoules) they are content

To whiſper. At the which, let no man wonder.

This man, with Lanthorne, dog, and buſh of thorne,

Preſenteth moone-ſhine. For if you will know,

By moone-shine did theſe Louers thinke no ſcorne

To meete at *Ninus* toombe, there, there to wooe :

This grizly beaſt (which Lyon hight by name)

The truſty *Thisby*, coming firſt by night,

Did ſcarre away, or rather did affright :

And as ſhe fled, her mantle ſhe did fall ;

Which Lion vile with bloody mouth did ſtaine.

Anon comes *Piramus*, ſweete youth and tall,

And finds his truſty *Thisbies* Mantle ſlaine ;

Whereat, with blade, with bloody blamefull blade,

He brauely broach his boiling bloody breaſt,

And *Thisby*, tarrying in Mulberry ſhade,

Hi

A Midſommer Nights Dreame.

His dagger drew and died. For all the reſt,

Let *Lyon, Moone-ſhine, Wall,* and Louers twaine,

At large diſcourſe, while here they do remaine.

    Theſ. I wonder if the Lyon be to ſpeake.

    Deme. No wonder, my Lord : one lion may, when

many Aſſes do.

Exit Lyon, Thisby, and Moone-ſhine.

    Wall. In this ſame Interlude it doth befall,

That I, one *Flute* (by name) preſent a wall :

And ſuch a wall, as I would haue you thinke,

That had in it a crannied hole or chinke :

Through which the Louers, *Piramus* and *Thisby,*

Did whiſper often, very ſecretly.

This lome, this roughcraſt, and this ſtone doth ſhow,

That I am that ſame wall ; the truth is ſo.

And this the cranny is, right and ſiniſter,

Through which the fearefull Louers are to whiſper.

    Theſ. Would you deſire lime and haire to ſpeak better ?

    Deme. It is the wittieſt paritition, that euer I heard diſ-

courſe, my Lord.

    Theſ. Piramus draws neere the wall, ſilence.

    Pir. O grim lookt night, ô night with hue ſo blacke,

O night, which euer art, when day is not :

O night, ô night, alacke, alacke, alacke,

I feare my *Thisbies* promiſe is forgot.

And

73

A Midſommer Nights Dreame.

And thou ô wall, ô ſweete, ô louely wall,

Shew me thy chinke, to blink through with mine eine.

Thanks courteous wall. *Ioue* ſhield thee well for this.

But what ſee I ? No *Thisby* do I ſee.

O wicked wall, though whom I ſee no bliſſe,

Curſt be thy ſtones, for thus deceiuing me.

    Theſ. The wall me-thinks being ſensible, ſhould curſe

againe.

    Pir. No in truth ſir, he ſhould not. *Deceiuing me,*

Is *Thisbies* cue ; ſhe is to enter now, and I am to ſpy

Her through the wall. You ſhall ſee it will fall

Pat as I told you ; yonder ſhe comes.   *Enter Thisbie.*

    Thiſ. O wall, full often haſt thou heard my mones,

For parting my faire *Piramus*, and me.

My cherry lips haue often kiſt thy ſtones ;

Thy ſtones with lime and haire knit now againe.

    Pyra. I ſee a voice ; now will I to the chinke,

To ſpy and I can heare my *Thisbies* face. *Thisby* ?

    Thiſ. My Loue thou art, my Loue I thinke.

    Pir. Thinke what thou wilt, I am thy Louers grace,

And like *Limander*, am I truſty ſtill.

    Thiſ. And I like *Helen*, till the fates me kill.

    Pir. Not *Shafalus* to *Procrus*, was ſo true.

    Thiſ. As *Shafalus* to *Procrus*, I to you.

    Pir. O kiſſe me through the hole of this vile wall.

                                                Thiſ.

Thiſ. I kiſſe the wals hole, not your lips at all.

Pir. Wilt thou at *Ninnies* tomb meete me ſtraightway ?

Thiſ. Tide life, tide death, I come without delay.

Wall. Thus haue I *Wall,* my part diſcharged ſo;
And being done, thus *Wall* away doth goe.

Du. Now is the Moon vſed betweene the two neighbors.

Deme. No remedy, my Lord, when wals are ſo wilfull, to
heare without warning.

Dutch. This is the ſillieſt ſtuffe that ere I heard.

Duke. The beſt in this kinde are but ſhadowes, and the
worſt are no worſe, if imagination amend them.

Dutch. It muſt be your imagination then, and not theirs.

Duke. If wee imagine no worſe of them then they of themſelues, they may paſſe for excellent men. Heere come two
noble beaſts, in a man and a Lyon.

Enter Lyon and Moone-ſhine,

Lyon. You Ladies, you (whoſe gentle hearts do feare
The ſmalleſt monſtrous mouſe that creepes on floore)
May now perchance, both quake and tremble heere,
When Lyon rough, in wildeſt rage doth roare.
Then know that I, as *Snug* the ioyner am
A Lyon fell, nor elſe no Lyons damme,
For if I ſhould, as Lyon come in ſtrife,
Into this place, t'were pitty on my life.

Duke. A very gentle beaſt, and of a good conſcience.

Deme.

A Midſommer Nights Dreame.

Deme. The very beſt at a beaſt, my Lord, that ere I ſaw.

Lyſ. This Lyon is a very Fox for his valour.

Duke. True, and a Gooſe for his diſcretion.

De. Not ſo my Lord. For his valour cannot carry his diſcretion ; and the Fox carries the gooſe.

Duke. His diſcretion I am ſure cannt carry his valour. For the Gooſe carries not the Fox. It is well ; leaue it to his diſcretion, and let vs hearken to the Moone.

Moon. This lanthorne doth the horned Moone preſent.

Deme. He ſhould haue worne the hornes on his head.

Duk. He is no creſcent, and his hornes are inuiſible, with-in the circumference.

Moone. This lanthorne doth the horned Moone preſent, My ſelge, the man ith'Moone do ſeeme to be.

Duke. This is the greateſt error of all the reſt ; the man ſhould be put into the Lanthorne. How is it elſe the man i'th Moone ?

Dem. He dares not come there for the candle. For you ſee, it is already in ſnuffe.   (change.

Dutch. I am weary of this Moone ; would he would

Duke. It appears by his ſmall light of diſcretion, that hee is in the wane : but yet in curteſie, in all reaſon, we muſt ſtay the time.

Lyſand. Proceed Moone.

Moone. All that I haue to ſay, is to tell you, that the Lan-

thorne

76

A Midſommer Nights Dreame.

thorne is the Moone ; I, the man in the Moone ; this thorne
buſh, my thorne buſh, and this dog, my dog.

Deme. Why all theſe ſhould nee in the Lanthorne : for they
are in the Moone. But ſilence, heere comes *Thisby.*

Enter Thisby.

Th. This is old *Ninies* tomb : wher's my loue ? *Lyon.* Oh.

Dem. Well roard Lyon.

Duke. Well runne *Thisby.*

Dutch. Well ſhoone *Moone.*   Truly the *Moone* ſhines
With a good grace.

Duke. Well mouz'd *Lyon.*

Dem. And then came *Piramus.*

Lyſ. And ſo the Lyon vaniſht.

Enter Piramus.

Pyr. Sweete Moone, I thank thee for thy ſunny beames,
I thanke thee Moone, for ſhining now ſo bright.
For by thy gracious, golden, glittering beames,
I truſt to take of trueſt *Thisbie* ſight.
But ſtay : ô ſpight ! but marke, poore knight,
What dreadfull dole is here ?
Eyes do you ſee ! how can it be !
O dainty ducke, ô deare !
Thy mantle good, what ſtaind with blood ?
Approach ye Furies fell,
O fates come, come, cut thred and thrum,

Quaile

77

A Midſommer Nights Dreame.

Quaile, cruſh, conclude, and quell.

    Duke. This paſſion, and the death of a deare friend would
go neere to make a man looke ſad.

    Dutch. Beſhrew my heart, but I pitty the man.

    Pir. O wherefore Nature, didſt thou Lyons frame ?
Since Lyon vilde hath heere deflour'd my deare ;
Which is, no, no, which was the faireſt dame
That liu'd, that lik't, that look't with cheere.
Come teares confound, out ſword and wound
The pap of *Pryamus* :
I, that left pap, where heart doth hop ;
Thus die I, thus, thus, thus.
Now am I dead, now am I fled, my foule, is in the sky,
Tongue loſe thy light, Moone take thy flight,
Now dye, dye, dye, dye, dye.

    Dem. No Die, but an ace for him ; for he is but one.

    Lyf. Leſſe then an ace man. For he is dead, he is
nothing.

    Duke. With the helpe of a Surgeon, he might yet reco-
uer and proue an aſſe.

    Dutch. How chance Moone-ſhine is gone before ?
Thisby comes backe, and finds her Louer.

    Duke. She will finde him by ſtar-light. Here ſhe comes,
and her paſſion ends the play.

    Dut. Me-thinkes ſhe ſhould not vſe a long one for ſuch

A Midſommer Nights Dreame.

a *Piramus* : I hope ſhe will be briefe.

    Dem. A Moth will turne the ballance, which *Piramus*,
Which *Thisbie* is the better : hee for a man, God warnd vs ;
ſhe for a woman, God bleſſe vs.

    Lyſ. She hath ſpied him already, with thoſe ſweete eies.

    Dem. And thus ſhe meanes, *videlicit.*

    Thiſ. Aſleepe my Loue ? What, dead my Doue ?
O *Piramus* ariſe,
Speake, ſpeake. Quite dumbe ? Dead, dead ? A toombe
Muſt couer thy ſweete eies.
Theſe lilly lips, this cheery noſe,
There yellow cowſlip cheekes
Are gone, are gone ; Louers make mone :
His eyes were greene as Leekes.
O ſiſters three, come, come to me,
With hands as pale as milke,
Lay them in gore, ſince you haue ſhore
With ſheeres, his thred of ſilke.
Tongue not a word, come truſty ſword,
Come blade, my breaſt imbrew :
And farwell friends, thus *Thisble* ends ;
Adieu, adieu, adieu.

    Duke. Moone-ſhine and Lyon are left to bury the dead.

    Deme. I, and Wall too.

    Lyon. No, I aſſure you the wall is downe, that parted

their

79

A Midſommer Nights Dreame.

their Fathers. Will it pleaſe you to ſee the Epilogue, or to
heare a Bergomask dance, betweene two of our company ?

 Duke. No Epilouge, I pray you ; for your play needs
no excuſe. Neuer excuſe ; for when the players are all
dead, there need none to be blamed. Marry, if he that
writ it, had plaid *Piramus,* and hang'd himſelfe in *This-*
bies garter, it would haue beene a fine Tragedy : a ſo it
is truely, and very notably diſcharg'd. But come, your
Burgomaske ; let your Epilouge alone.
The iron tongue of midnight hath tolde twelue.
Louers to bed, tis almoſt Fairy time.
I feare we ſhall out-ſleepe the comming morne,
As much as we this night haue ouer-watcht.
This palpable groſſe play hath well beguil'd
The heauy gate of night. Sweet friends to bed.
A fortnight hold we hold this ſolemnity,
In nightly Reuels, and new iolluty.   *Exeunt.*

Enter Pucke.

Puck. Now the hungry Lyons rores,
And the Wolfe beholds the Moone ;
Whilſt the heauy ploughman ſnores,
All with weary taske fore-done.
Now the waſted brands do glow,
Whilſt the ſcritch-owle, ſcritching loud,
Puts the wretch that lies in woe,

In

A Midſommer Nights Dreame.

In remembrance of a ſhrowd.
Now it is the time of night,
That the graues, all gaping wide,
Euery one lets forth his ſpright,
In the Churchway paths to glide.
And we Fairies, that do runnne,
But the triple *Hecates* teame,
From the preſence of the Sunne,
Following darkneſſe like a dreame,
Now are frollicke ; not a Mouſe
Shall diſturbe this hallowed houſe.
I am ſent with broome before,
That you haue but ſlumbred heere,
While this weake and idle theame,
No more yeelſing but a dream,
Gentles, do not reprehend.
If you pardon, we will mend.
And as I am an honeſt *Pucke,*
If we haue vnearned lucke,
Now to ſcape the Serpents tongue,
We will make amends ere long :
Elſe the *Pucke* a lyar call.
So good night vnto you all.
Giue me your hands, if we be friends,
And *Robin* ſhall reſtore amends.

ᚠINIS.

Jabberwoke Pocket Occult Collection

CRYSTAL GAZING *by Frater Achad*

Thus, it is hoped, all will be satisfied; and should their satisfaction be equal to that of the Author at this opportunity to herald the Light – however faintly – of the Ultimate Crystalline Sphere.

ISBN: 978-1-954873-36-0
$ 11.00 USD
FraterAchadCrystalGazing.com

HEAVENLY BRIDEGROOMS *by Ida Craddock*

"One of the most remarkable human documents ever produced... This book is of incalculable value to every student of Occult matters. No Magick library is complete without it" – A.C.

ISBN: 978-1-954873-21-6
$ 14.00 USD
HeavenlyBridegrooms.com

MOONCHILD *by Aleister Crowley*

The cattiest & messiest novel from the transcriber of the Wickedest Man in England. Hiding behind the guise of fiction, Moonchild is the Beast's platform to slander his many nemeses inside the spiritualist circles of London.

ISBN: 978-1-954873-53-7
$ 19.00 USD /
AleisterCrowleyMoonchild.com

THE KYBALION *by Three Initiates*

There is no portion of the occult teachings which have been so closely guarded as the fragments of the Hermetic Teachings, the Great Central Sun of Occultism, whose rays have illuminated the teachings promulgated since a time.

ISBN: 978-1-954873-08-7
$ 14.00 USD
ThreeInitiatesKybalion.com

THE SO-CALLED OCCULT *by Carl Jung*

A 20-year-old Carl Jung attends his cousin's seances leading to a psychological investigation of haunting, witch-sleeps, and delicious bliss that unravels int obsession.

ISBN: 978-1-954873-39-1
$ 14.00 USD
TheSoCalledOccult.com

THE GREAT GOD PAN *by Arthur Machen*

A classic of pagan horror that follows the trail of destruction left in the wake of a mysterious socialite, as she serves the will of her shadowy, horned benefactor.

ISBN: 978-1-954873-35-3
$14.00 USD
AllHailPan.com

THE WITCH CULT *by Margaret Murray*

Firsthand accounts of a pre-Christian witch cult that worshiped the Horned God of fertility—whose Christian persecutors referred to him as the Devil—and the nocturnal rites performed at the witches' Sabbath.

ISBN: 978-1-954873-33-9
$19.00 USD
TheWitchCult.com

THE BOOK OF LIES *by Frater Perdurabo*

A collection of falsehoods from Dionysus, received by the mysterious Frater Perdurabo and the Scarlet Woman LAYLAH. This wicked book is said to contain within its pages the secret truth of the universe . . . readers beware.

ISBN: 978-1-954873-37-7
$14.00 USD
FaleslyCalledBreaks.com

A MIDSOMMAR NIGHT'S DREAM *by William Shakespeare*

The timeless ethereal tale of four Lovers who wander too close to the games of Titania and Oberon, the Faerie Queen and King, and their encounters with the archetypal Tickster Puck and all the fantastical beings whom inhabit the woodland realm.

ISBN: 978-1-954873-54-4
$11.00 USD
MidsommarNightsDream.com

SATAN: A NOVEL *by Mark Twain*

The greatest and final novel from the master of American fiction, Mark Twain's fable of an angelic visitation in the Austrian countryside reveals the solipsism of its author, and his belief of the unreality of our collective dream.

ISBN: 978-1-954873-59-9
$16.00 USD
MarkTwainSatan.com

JABBERWOKE © MMXXI

Wholesale Inquiries:
contact@jabberwokebooks.com

www.ingramcontent.com/pod-product-compliance
Lightning Source LLC
Chambersburg PA
CBHW021333060726
47591CB00006B/2001